THE SUCCESS FORMULA

FOR PERSONAL GROWTH

2,000 Motivational Quotes
Strategies and Advice From
500 Super Successful People

Jerry Bruckner

Copyright

The Success Formula For Personal Growth

Copyright © 2010 by Gerald (Jerry) D. Bruckner.

ISBN: 978-0-615-35550-4

All rights reserved. No part of this publication may be reproduced, distributed, or transmitted in any form or by any means, or stored in a database or retrieval system, without prior written permission of the Publisher.

BRIJU Publishing
P.O. Box 2764
Stamford, CT 06906

First eBook Edition: January 2010

First Printed Edition February 2010

The Author welcomes reader feedback about this book.

To contact the Author or send feedback about the book, please send an email to: SuccessFormulaForPersonalGrowth@yahoo.com

Dedication

This book is dedicated to the two most beautiful and spirited people I know: my wife Judy and our daughter Brianna. Each moment shared with you is a joy.

Your Loving Husband and Father,

Jerry Bruckner

Contents

1. Introduction To The Success Formula 1
2. What Can The Success Formula Do For You? 5
3. What Is Success? 16
4. Learn How To Succeed From Successful People 22
5. You Have The Power To Change And Improve Your Life 24
6. Create The Life You Want To Live And Have Remembered 30
7. Different Results Require A Different Approach 33
8. Take Responsibility For Your Life 35
9. Don't Make Excuses, Complain, Or Blame Anyone Or Anything For Your Present Circumstances 42
10. Your Choices Have Consequences 46
11. Your Good And Bad Habits Can Lead To Or Prevent Success, Happiness And Fulfillment 51
12. You Become What You Think About Most Of The Time 54
13. Believe It's Possible You Can Accomplish Your Dreams! 59
14. Live With Passion, Do What You Love To Do 64
15. Aspire To Achieve Your Greatest Ambitions And Dreams, Think BIG! 68
16. Your Personal Development Is The Key To Become Happy, Successful And Fulfilled 72
17. Invest Time Every Day To Learn And Improve Yourself 74
18. Practice Self-Control And Self-Discipline To Control Your Thoughts, Emotions And Actions 80
19. Improve Your Attention, Awareness, Focus And Concentration To Excel At What You Do 82

20. Preparation Is The Iceberg People Do Not See When They Notice You Are Successful 86

21. Conduct An Honest Self-Assessment 90

22. Develop Your Vision Statement, Live Your Life On Purpose Not By Accident 93

23. Set Major Goals That Give Your Life Purpose, Direction And Meaning 96

24. Create A Written Plan To Achieve Your Goals And Reach Your Vision 106

25. Commitment: Make An Unshakeable Promise To Yourself To Achieve Your Goals 108

26. Expect Success 111

27. Remain Flexible And Adapt As You Execute Your Plan 114

28. Don't Procrastinate To Start On Your Goals And Focus Time Every Day To Work On Them 118

29. Track And Measure Your Progress Towards Achieving Your Goals 125

30. Always Do Your Absolute Best! 127

31. Be Enthusiastic About Everything You Do! 131

32. Be Proactive, Take Initiative, Be A Go-Getter 134

33. Take Calculated Risks 137

34. Believe In Yourself! Self-Respect, Self-Esteem, Self-Confidence 140

35. Have A Positive Attitude, Be Optimistic 149

36. Never Quit! Be Mentally Tough, Determined, Patient, Tenacious, Persistent And Be Relentlessly Resourceful 154

37. Figure Out How To Inspire And Motivate Yourself 167

38. Have Supportive Friends 169

39. Avoid Unsuccessful And Unsupportive People 171
40. Make Decisive Decisions 173
41. Problems Present Opportunities
    For You To Learn And Grow 176
42. Learn From Your Setbacks And Mistakes 179
43. Always Do The Right Thing 186
44. Change Before You Have To,
    The World And Your Life Do Not Stand Still 188
45. Destroy Your Limiting Beliefs And Toxic Self-Talk
    To Stop Holding Yourself Back 191
46. Conquer Your Fear 197
47. Reject Rejection! 203
48. Eliminate Your Unsuccessful Thoughts And Actions 205
49. Learn To Turn Off Stress And Perform Well
    Under Pressure 207
50. Get Comfortable Being Uncomfortable,
    Go Outside Your "Comfort Zone" To Improve 209
51. Meditate To Reduce Stress, Calm Your Mind,
    Improve Your Focus And Concentration 212
52. Use Visualizations To Train Your Mind
    To Accomplish Anything 214
53. Use Affirmations To Fire-Up Your Positive Attitude 218
54. Create And Celebrate Your Victory Journal 220
55. Communicate Effectively: Be Likeable, Connect, Establish
    Rapport And Build Trust To Get Your Message Across 222
56. Persuasion And Sales: All Communication Involves Selling
    Yourself And Your Ideas To Others 229

57. Be Assertive When Necessary, Ask For And Say
    What You Want, Stick Up For Yourself 233

58. Build Your Personal Network 234

59. Treat Everyone Like A Customer,
    Provide World Class Service 236

60. Master Your Elevator Pitch And Personal Brand
    To Stand Out And Differentiate Yourself 239

61. Teamwork: You Must Work Well And Get Along With
    People To Accomplish Your Goals 241

62. Leadership: Respect And Value People
    To Inspire Them To Do Their Best 244

63. Don't Waste Your Time Or Let Anyone Else Waste It,
    Be Organized And Prioritize 252

64. Learn From Your Past, Live In The Present,
    Plan For Your Future 261

65. Look For Opportunities
    And How To Take Advantage Of Them 264

66. Have An Open Mind To New Ideas
    And Don't Let Ideas Escape 268

67. Be Creative: Invent And Innovate,
    Look For New And Better Ways To Do Things 271

68. Personal Character Counts 274

69. Be Couragous 277

70. Be Loving, Never Neglect Your Family 279

71. Be Honest, Have Integrity, Always Keep Your Promises 281

72. Be Happy And Lighten Up, Enjoy A Good Laugh 284

73. Be Charitable, Give Back, Be Generous 288

74. Be Kind 290

75. Be Respectful 292

76. Be Grateful 293

77. Be Humble 294

78. Be Forgiving 295

79. Don't Envy Or Be Jealous 298

80. Release Your Anger 299

81. Exercise: Sound Mind In A Sound Body 301

82. Money Isn't Everything,
    But It's Right Up There With Oxygen 303

83. How To Increase Your Luck 307

84. The Power Of Personal Momentum 309

85. Want More Out Of Life?
    Be A Little Restless And Discontented 311

86. Ask Lots Of Questions 313

About The Author 316

Index……………………………………………………....317

1

Introduction To The Success Formula

No one has yet found *The Elixir for Immortality*, *The Fountain of Youth* or a *Love Potion*, but there is a time proven **Success Formula** that anyone can use to become successful and lead a happy and fulfilled life.

The Success Formula is not magical. You cannot become successful by simply wishing for it. The real *Success Formula* has been used for thousands of years to achieve success in any area of human activity.

The Success Formula consists of specific personal actions, habits, internal belief systems, principles and strategies, that are easy to understand, and can be applied by anyone who has the desire, commitment, courage, discipline, determination and persistence to learn these *success lessons* and put them into practice in their daily life.

The elements of *The Success Formula* can be thought of as success lessons which must be learned for someone to become successful.

There are three ways to learn anything:

1. Personal experience and use trial and error. This is the most time consuming way to learn.

2. Observe, speak to and interact with someone else who has already learned the subject, if you are fortunate enough to do so.

3. Read and reflect upon the written wisdom and experiences of other people.

The third method allows anyone to learn and benefit from the lessons others have spent time to learn and write about, so it saves you the time of trying to figure out what works, and it allows you to learn at your own pace. This book is based on this approach to learning.

Brian Tracy
- "No one lives long enough to learn everything they need to learn starting from scratch. To be successful, we absolutely, positively have to find people who have already paid the price to learn the things that we need to learn to achieve our goals."

Confucius
- "By three methods we may learn wisdom: First, by reflection, which is noblest; Second, by imitation, which is easiest; and third by experience, which is the bitterest."

Euripides
- "Some wisdom you must learn from one who's wise."

Sam Levenson
- "You must learn from the mistakes of others. You can't possibly live long enough to make them all yourself."

Isaac Newton
- "If I have seen farther it is by standing on the shoulders of giants."

Voltaire
- "Is there anyone so wise as to learn by the experience of others?"

Wendell Barry
- "It is not from ourselves that we learn to be better than we are."

The Success Formula's success lessons are presented in this book by using a unique and entertaining approach to use over 2,000 byte-sized, highly inspirational, informative and easy to read and understand *quotations* from over 500 of the most successful and influential people, from Ancient times up until today, in which these *success experts* explain their views on the keys to become successful.

The quotations of these *success experts* contain compacted wisdom, experience, common sense and teachings that demonstrate that all

Introduction to the Success Formula

successful people share a common way to think and act that has been used time and time again to change and improve people's lives.

The lessons in *The Success Formula* empower people to accomplish whatever they desire and to become successful and lead happy and fulfilled lives.

Throughout history, people have agreed that short *quotations* are a powerful, highly effective and efficient method to communicate wisdom and successful experience in a few words.

Benjamin Disraeli
- "The wisdom of the wise and the experience of the ages are perpetuated by quotations."

Marlene Dietrich
- "I love quotations because it is a joy to find thoughts one might have, beautifully expressed with much authority by someone recognizably wiser than oneself."

Sophocles
- "A short saying often contains much wisdom."

The Talmud
- "A quotation at the right moment is like bread to the famished."

Winston Churchill
- "It is a good thing for an uneducated man to read books of quotations."

The entire *Success Formula* consisting of its *success lessons* is listed in the Table of Contents.

A lot of thought has gone into the order that the lessons are presented, and the specific quotations chosen for each lesson, so that the quotations and lessons flow together to produce an entertaining, easy to read and understand presentation of *The Success Formula*.

It is strongly encouraged that you please read the lessons in the order they are presented and to please not skip any of them.

THE SUCCESS FORMULA FOR PERSONAL GROWTH

Each success lesson contains a brief overview of its main points which is presented as concise statements written by this author in the same format of a compact quotation. This is followed by a list of quotations from many success experts listed alphabetically by the success expert's name.

Each success lesson contains many similar but slightly different quotations. The reason for this is that it is commonly known that different people respond to and learn information differently.

If only a small number of quotations was presented, those particular quotations might not *register* and *strike a conceptual or emotional nerve* with the reader.

By including multiple quotations, each of which communicates a slightly different piece of the particular lesson, or states it in a slightly different way, the reader will find one or more quotations that clearly communicate the *messages* of that lesson and resonates on a conceptual and emotional level with them.

Also, because we know that repetition increases learning, the messages of that lesson will be reinforced by reading all of the related quotations. In effect, the reader is immersed in the concepts of the lesson.

To summarize, the success lessons in this book that make up *The Success Formula* contain the proven principles and strategies used by all successful people, which, if you take the time to learn, absorb, and create habits to put them into daily action, will empower and inspire you to:

- Change and improve your life.
- Rebuild yourself from the inside out.
- Enhance your abilities to think, communicate and live.
- Achieve your goals and dreams.
- Enjoy a happy, successful and rewarding life.

2

What Can The Success Formula Do For You?

The Success Formula presented in this book provides you with a wide ranging guide to the thinking and actions that lead to achieving personal growth and success, such as becoming an expert communicator in addition to training your mind to maximize its positive output and to eliminate your negative limitations that are holding you back.

The Success Formula also addresses time management and problem solving skills, as well as much more.

In short, the goal of this book is to provide you with a holistic view of personal development to empower you to change and improve, with the goal to achieve personally rewarding success, happiness and fulfillment in your life.

The success lessons in this book are all based on common sense and the application of hard work.

There is no lesson in this book that teaches that you can instantly change your life and have anything and everything you want, by simply closing your eyes and clicking your heels together three times while asking the Universe to give it to you; and that the Universe will then magically understand your request and will attract the object of your desire into your life.

Although I do not believe that making wishes to the Universe without any other effort on your part will get you what you wish for, I do believe that you have an almost unlimited power to believe in yourself, and your belief, coupled with your purposeful action and other skills and habits explained in this book can get you what you want.

Whether we call your power self-esteem, self-respect, self-worth or self-confidence, this power fuels your positive internal thinking, inspiration, motivation and commitment, and it energizes your external drive to enable you to conceive what you want in life, to believe you are worthy of having it and that you can obtain it, and it empowers you to tenaciously focus and work hard to achieve what you want, and never quit trying to accomplish your goals.

A person who believes in themselves can achieve anything they are capable of doing, that they decide is something they want to do, and they are willing to pay the price to do it. For example, no matter how much you believe in yourself you cannot flap your arms and fly in the sky like a bird. But if you want to be a Doctor and are willing to dedicate many years of your life to hard study and school (pay the price) you can set your sights on this goal.

There are several techniques covered in this book by which you can increase your belief in yourself, such as getting into the habit to set and complete your personal goals, use active visualization and use emotionally charged affirmations. There are also other techniques to reduce any limiting beliefs and thoughts that you may have that eat away at your belief in yourself and hold you back.

No matter what age you are now, you can decide to improve yourself and get more out of life. If you are already somewhat successful you can become more successful. The key point is that you always have the ability to choose to improve yourself to the best of your ability at whatever point you are in life.

The simple truth is that if you believe you can change and improve, and you commit yourself to personal development and to

WHAT CAN THE SUCCESS FORMULA DO FOR YOU?

achieve your goals, you will accomplish more in life than if you did not try to change and improve and work to achieve your goals.

It's not enough to only *want* to improve. You need to know *what* to improve in your life and *how* to equip yourself to play and win in the game of life the same way other successful people do.

It's a funny thing, we spend most of our time in life understanding the world *outside* of us and we spend very little time examining the world *inside* of us.

Only by understanding what is going on inside of you, and how you think, will you be able to improve and be a success at whatever you aspire to be and have in life. And that's exactly what this book is designed to help you to do.

What's in it for you to read this book?

- You will **learn** how successful people think, **to maximize your positive thoughts and actions** and **eliminate** your **limiting thoughts, fears, anxieties, doubts and unproductive behaviors that hold you back.**

- You will **learn** techniques **to become a masterful communicator** to enable you to *connect* **with people to create rewarding personal relationships and effective work relationships. People will enjoy listening to you and be persuaded by what you say.**

- You will **learn** effective techniques **to determine your life's purpose, set meaningful and realistic goals, conquer procrastination and improve yourself every day.**

- You will get **certainty** that you know what to learn and do to improve your life.

- You will have **security** that these principals and concepts will work to enable you to obtain what you want.

- You will develop **control** over your life.

- You will have **pride** knowing you are following a path that will lead to success.

- You will increase your **self-esteem** and **self-respect** and **feel good about yourself** for making the decision and to take the effort to learn about how you can achieve success and to start to bring your success closer.

- You will be **happy** that you have committed to follow a path of self-improvement to become the best you can be.

- You will have **confidence** that you can become a winner in life!

The truth is, that *The Success Formula:* how to achieve your maximum personal development, growth and personal success in any area of your life, is a process that all successful people follow.

It involves a particular way of *thinking, communicating,* and *living* that can be learned by anyone who *believes in themself*, has an *unshakeable commitment* to improve their life, is willing to *change* and *learn*, takes *constant purposeful action* to *achieve* their *meaningful goals*, and *adjusts and learns from setbacks*.

There are other strategies explained in this book but these are the core concepts to become successful.

In order to identify the common traits and practices of all successful people to write this book, I read the writings and watched the available presentations of over 500 very successful people from Ancient times up to today.

WHAT CAN THE SUCCESS FORMULA DO FOR YOU?

My research included people in all areas of human activity that are universally recognized as having achieved great success, including:

- Great Ancient Thinkers and Leaders such as Buddha, Jesus, Moses, Krishna, Confucius, Aristotle, Socrates and Emperor Marcus Aurelius.

- Pioneering Inventors such as Thomas Edison and Henry Ford.

- Industrial Tycoons such as Andrew Carnegie and John D. Rockefeller.

- Brilliant Scientists such as Madam Curie and Albert Einstein.

- Acclaimed Writers such as Mark Twain and Ernest Hemingway.

- Magnificent Artists such as Michelangelo and Leonardo da Vinci.

- Amazing Athletes such as boxer Mohamed Ali, tennis player John McEnroe and basketball player Michael Jordan.

- Winning Sports coaches such as Vince Lombardi, John Wooden and Pat Riley.

- Spectacular Entertainers such as Sylvester Stallone.

- Modern Business Titans such as Bill Gates, Steve Jobs, Jack Welch, Donald Trump and Oprah Winfrey.

- Incredible Martial artists such as Bruce Lee.

As I reviewed the writings and presentations from all of the people I studied, I discovered that these very successful people shared many of the same beliefs and practices as to what it takes for a person to be successful – it was a *Success Formula*.

I analyzed the *Success Formula* and broke it down into the lessons in this book. Each of these lessons can improve your life, and together they provide the real *secret* to personal growth and success.

Who can benefit from reading this book?

- Employees
- Salespeople
- Entrepreneurs
- Students
- Unemployed or Downsized People
- Leaders and Managers
- Parents
- Athletes, Artists and Entertainers

In short, anyone of any age who wants more out of life and is concerned about their future will benefit from reading, learning, absorbing and developing habits based on the *success lessons* in this book.

You are capable of deciding your own destiny; the question is: "Which path will you chose?"

Honestly ask yourself the following questions:
- Are you satisfied with your life?
- Do you feel you are capable of much more than you presently have?
- Do you want to change and improve yourself and achieve success?
- Do you want to provide a better life for your loved ones?
- Do you want to make yourself more valuable to an employer or increase your ability to have your own business?

A very important question for you to ask yourself:

<u>Is it worth it for you to spend a few hours to read this book and possibly learn how to change and improve your life?</u>

If your answer is "No," then I thank you for your time and wish you well. On the other hand, if your answer is "Yes," then I congratulate

WHAT CAN THE SUCCESS FORMULA DO FOR YOU?

you on taking an important step to change and improve your life for the better.

What you will learn in this book will give you the knowledge, tools and strategies to change yourself from ordinary to extraordinary.

That may sound like an impossible task, until you stop to think about the following question:

What is an extraordinary person?

An extraordinary person is someone who consistently does the things ordinary people can't do, or won't do, such as committing themselves to self-improvement and setting and achieving meaningful goals.

If you want to succeed you need to start thinking like successful people and live your life with the following:

- A commitment to constant and continuous **change**.
- A commitment to constant and continuous **growth**.
- A commitment to constant and continuous **improved performance**.

The power of believing in yourself and taking smart determined action to achieve your goals, and putting into habitual practice other principles and keys in this book are the time proven *Success Formula* anyone can use to change and improve any area in their life.

- The truth is, anyone can succeed if they truly want to.
- This book leads you step by step through *The Success Formula*.
- You can change who and what you are by what you put into your mind.
- What you put in your mind changes your thinking.
- When you change your thinking you change your actions.

- When you change your actions you change your future.

Think about where your life is now. Like many people you may be sad, bored, worried, fearful, anxious, stressed out or angry with things in your life, and frustrated because you feel you are not living up to your potential.

Now imagine what your life could be, if you learn and absorb the information in this book and take action to improve yourself to change the way you think, plan, and act, and to become an excellent communicator.

Do you remember a time in your life when you thought all things were possible and you could succeed in life, and then, over the years that feeling faded away? The success lessons in this book are based on common sense.

By reading these success principles over and over with *emotional commitment* you can retrain your mind to renew that inspirational way of thinking and communicating.

Take a minute and consider your current life. What are the things you want to achieve and have, and what are the things you do not want or like in your life and wish you could change? You can program yourself to change your life and achieve your goals.

Think of yourself as a biological computer that runs software in your mind and heart that produces the outcome of your life. Of course, every human is not a computer that is running software inside of them, but the comparison is very illuminating. The better a computer's hardware the better its performance, and the more software, the more the computer can be used to do.

If a computer has damaged hardware or the software has a virus or bugs it will produce inaccurate results, and will not perform well.

WHAT CAN THE SUCCESS FORMULA DO FOR YOU?

Human beings have similar problems. If your software (your thoughts and feelings) have a virus or bugs, or you don't have a high performance operating system or the right software, you will have defective thinking, negative and limiting beliefs, values, fears and emotions, and your actions and performance will not be the best they can be.

The result, is that it is unlikely you will be able to set the right goals, and even if you do, you won't have the ability to accomplish them.

A computer can be fixed or upgraded, and the truth is your thinking can be fixed and upgraded (retrained by you).

If you read this book and make an honest and unshakeable commitment to yourself to understand the concepts in this book, that successful people have known and used from ancient times up to our modern time, you can improve and start to rewire your software (your thoughts and feelings) for high performance.

I'm not trying to sell you on anything more than to encourage you to believe in yourself and that it's worth it for you to learn the time proven concepts in this book to improve your life.

I will earn money by the sale of this book but, I will earn more in happiness knowing that I have helped you to improve your life the same way I learned after many obstacles and setbacks, to improve my own life. If I can do it, so can you.

I do not know you, we have never met. You have picked up this book and read this far because you are concerned about your life. You know you can accomplish more than you have, and you want to improve. I congratulate you for taking the time to seek knowledge that will help you.

Your present circumstances establish your *starting point*, but they do not determine your *destination*. Where you are today will very quickly become where you've been. So keep your eyes focused on the future -- where you want to go -- instead of on the past -- where you've been.

Whether you are twenty or fifty years old, or younger or older, there is an undeniable truth that you have the rest of your life to live and it's up to you to decide how you will live it.

There are people who succeed while very young and others succeed when they are much older after they have found out what they want and don't want in their life.

It's your choice and decision what you will do with the rest of your life. True success is accepting who you are right now, and committing yourself to become the absolute best you can be.

To become successful we must eliminate everything about us that leads to being unsuccessful and replace them with things that will make us successful.

Learn from the experts because they have already traveled the road you want to drive on. They have done the examination and you can learn from it.

Success is not an accident or luck; it is a skill that can be learned by anyone. The sooner you learn the skill of success, the sooner you will achieve what you were destined to accomplish in life.

A core concept in this book is that successful people develop their ability to *lead themselves* to accomplish whatever they want out of life.

Everyone can be a leader. Being a leader doesn't require that you have followers. It means that you live life on your terms, you don't settle, you see things as they are, you are honest with yourself and you constantly strive to improve and to achieve your goals.

Being a leader means you see the challenges but you don't make them worse than they are by thinking you can't accomplish what you want. You develop whatever skills you need to succeed, such as learning

What Can the Success Formula Do for You?

to think like a champion, and to be an excellent communicator who people will enjoy speaking with, and they will trust and believe what you say.

I know in my mind and heart that the success lessons in *The Success Formula* contain truths that anyone can follow to improve their life. I sincerely hope you will take the time to read and learn these truths, and create habits to put them into daily practice to create success and fulfillment in your own life.

You can succeed if you give it your absolute best!

3

What Is Success?

Jerry's Tips:

- There is no one definition of success that everyone can agree on but that doesn't mean that we can't do our best, to become our best and achieve our best to provide the best we can for ourselves and our loved ones.

- The way to be successful is to figure out how you can provide results or value for people, and then develop your ability to do that, and profits will come your way.

- Success is enlightened self-interest. By taking care of yourself you acquire the resources to take care of your family and the larger community.

- Success is not a destination; it is a continuous journey of striving toward your important goals that never ends.

- Success is a process - a way of living, not a result. But remember, results count.

- Success is measured by the accumulation of wealth, power, status, and property but remember happiness does not come from just having more things.

- Success does not happen by accident. It is the result of a determined process to decide what you want to achieve and do in your life, what the steps are you that need to do to achieve and accomplish it, and to constantly learn and to keep trying till you get what you want.

Arnold H. Glasow
- "Success isn't a result of spontaneous combustion. You must set yourself on fire."

What is Success?

Arthur Ashe
- "Success is a journey, not a destination. The doing is often more important than the outcome."

Blaise Pascal
- "It is the fight alone that pleases us, not the victory."

Brian Tracy
- "Successful people are always looking for opportunities to help others. Unsuccessful people are always asking 'What's in it for me?'"

Bob Dylan
- "A person is a success if they get up in the morning and gets to bed at night and in between does what he wants to do."

Cecil B. De Mille
- "The person who makes a success of living is the one who sees his goal steadily and aims for it unswervingly. That is dedication."

Christopher Morley
- "There is only one success—to be able to spend your life in you own way."

Deepak Chopra
- "There are many aspects to success; material wealth is only one component. Success is a journey, not a destination."
- "Success also includes good health, energy and enthusiasm for life, fulfilling relationships, creative freedom, emotional and psychological stability, a sense of well-being and peace of mind."
- "Success in life could be defined as the continued expansion of happiness and the progressive realization of worthy goals."
- "Success is a process that requires hard work."

Earl Nightingale
- "Success is the progressive realization of a worthy ideal."
- "If a person is working toward a predetermined goal and knows where they are going that person is successful. If a person does not know which direction they want to go in life, then that person is a failure."

THE SUCCESS FORMULA FOR PERSONAL GROWTH

- "Success is not the result of making money; making money is the result of success and success is in direct proportion to our service."

- "We will receive not what we idly wish for but what we justly earn. Our rewards will always be in exact proportion to our service." Increase your service to others and your rewards will increase in proportion."

Elbert Hubbard
- "He has achieved success who has lived well, laughed often and loved much."

Greg Norman
- "You only get out of it what you put into it. If you are a sheep in this world, you're not going to get much out of it."

Jim Rohn
- "Success is something you attract by the person you become."

- "Success is doing ordinary things extraordinarily well."

- "Success is neither magical or mysterious. Success is the natural consequence of consistently applying the basic fundamentals."

- "Success is steady progress toward one's personal goals."

John Wooden
- "Success, to me, is peace of mind, which is a direct result of self satisfaction in knowing you made the effort to become the best of which you're capable. Success is coming as close as possible to reaching your maximum potential at whatever task you're involved in."

Les Brown
- "Help others achieve their dreams and you will achieve yours."

Mohandas Gandhi
- "Satisfaction does not come with achievement, but with effort. Full effort is full victory."

What is Success?

Nido Qubein

- "Your value in the marketplace is determined by the size of problems you are capable of solving for other people and how easy it is to find someone else who can do what you do."

- "You can have anything you want providing you have:
  1. Clarity of vision about what you want to achieve in life,
  2. A solid strategy (goals and a plan) to get you from where you are now to where you want to be,
  3. Employ practical systems habitually to do meaningful things everyday to accomplish your goals, and
  4. Consistent execution."

Og Mandino

- "Failure is man's inability to reach his goals in life, whatever they may be."

Orison Swett Marden

- "The quality of your work, in the long run, is the deciding factor on how much your services are valued by the world."

Pablo Picasso

- "Our goals can only be reached through a vehicle of a plan, in which we must fervently believe, and upon which we must vigorously act. There is no other route to success."

Paul Meyer

- "Crystallize your goals. Make a plan for achieving them and set yourself a deadline. Then, with supreme confidence, determination and disregard for obstacles and other people's criticisms, carry out your plan."

Steve Bennett

- "A person adds value to a company by being a content expert or a facilitative leader. ... Be clear on how they add value on both of those fronts. Even more important, I would say, 'Have a passion for your job, or you won't excel.' The world is very competitive, so figure out what your passion is. If you want to have a great career, align it with your passion and then figure out how you can add value."

THE SUCCESS FORMULA FOR PERSONAL GROWTH

Tony Robbins
- "My definition of success is to live your life in a way that causes you to feel a ton of pleasure and very little pain and because of your lifestyle, have the people around you feel a lot more pleasure than they do pain."

- "Success comes from taking the initiative and following up... persisting... eloquently expressing the depth of your love. What simple action could you take today to produce a new momentum toward success in your life?"

- "Success is doing what you want to do, when you want, where you want, with whom you want, as much as you want."

- "Success is a commitment to personal growth on a daily basis."

- "It is not what we get. But who we become, what we contribute... that gives meaning to our lives."

- "The truth of the matter is that there's nothing you can't accomplish if:
  1. You clearly decide what it is that you're absolutely committed to achieving,
  2. You're willing to take massive action,
  3. You notice what's working or not, and
  4. You continue to change your approach until you achieve what you want, using whatever life gives you along the way."

Vince Lombardi
- "A man can be as great as he wants to be. If you believe in yourself and have the courage, the determination, the dedication, the competitive drive and if you are willing to sacrifice the little things in life and pay the price for the things that are worthwhile, it can be done."

Will Rogers
- "If you want to be successful, it's just this simple. Know what you are doing. Love what you are doing. And believe in what you are doing."

Zig Ziglar
- "You can have anything in life you want, if you will just help other people get what they want."

WHAT IS SUCCESS?

- "Success is the maximum utilization of the ability that you have."

- "Success means doing the best we can with what we have."

- "Success is the doing, not the getting; in the trying, not the triumph."

- "Success is a personal standard, reaching for the highest that is in us, becoming all that we can be."

- "You do not pay the price of success, you enjoy the price of success."

- "Success is not a destination, it's a journey."

- "I believe that being successful means having a balance of success stories across the many areas of your life. You can't truly be considered successful in your business life if your home life is in shambles."

4

Learn How To Succeed From Successful People

Jerry's Tips:

- Hang around successful people and learn from them.

- Do whatever you can to associate yourself with successful people in whatever field you want to succeed in.

- Find a mentor who has succeeded in the field you want to do.

- A successful person will give you confidence to pursue your goal and will not tell you something you want to do can not be done or laugh at your ideas because successful people are attracted to big ideas and big challenges.

- Watch what unsuccessful people do and make sure you don't do it.

Anonymous
- "Mentor: Someone whose hindsight can become your foresight."

Brian Tracy
- "No one lives long enough to learn everything they need to learn starting from scratch. To be successful, we absolutely, positively have to find people who have already paid the price to learn the things that we need to learn to achieve our goals."

Les Brown
- "If you want to be rich watch what rich people do everyday and do it. And watch what poor people do and don't do it."

LEARN HOW TO SUCCEED FROM SUCCESSFUL PEOPLE

Robert Kiyosaki
- "If you want to go somewhere, it is best to find someone who has already been there."

Roy H. Williams
- "A smart man makes a mistake, learns from it, and never makes that mistake again. But a wise man finds a smart man and learns from him how to avoid the mistake altogether."

Tony Robbins
- "If you want to be successful, find someone who has achieved the results you want and copy what they do and you'll achieve the same results."

Warren Buffet
- "It's better to hang out with people better than you. Pick out associates whose behavior is better than yours and you'll drift in that direction."

5

You Have The Power To Change And Improve Your Life

Jerry's Tips:

- Today, you have 100% of the rest of your life to live to its fullest!

- No matter how difficult your life may be now you can turn it around and learn how to succeed if you are willing to work hard for it.

- You are not a rock -- you are a person. You have the power to change, improve and succeed in any area of your life if you really want to.

- If you are somewhat successful now you can learn to become much more successful.

- You are in the driver's seat of your life and you can decide to keep driving down the road you're on, or you can turn and go a new direction whenever you want to.

- Regardless of your past or present circumstances you can set a better direction today and become successful.

- You are never too young or old to change and improve.

- A little change in your thoughts and actions can make a big difference in your life.

- Forgive yourself for all of your past mistakes and vow to change and improve yourself.

- You must believe with all your spirit that what you have done in life so far and what you are doing now is not as important as what you now want to accomplish.

YOU HAVE THE POWER TO CHANGE AND IMPROVE YOUR LIFE

- To change your life is really very simple; all you have to do is ask yourself: 'What can I do right now to improve my life?' And then start to do it – NOW!

You Have The Power To Change And Improve Your Life.

Dr. Maxwell Maltz
- "Within you right now is the power to do things you never dreamed possible. This power becomes available to you just as soon as you can change your beliefs."

Dale Carnegie
- "We all have possibilities we don't know about. We can do things we don't even dream we can do."

H. Jackson Brown, Jr.
- "Never underestimate your power to change yourself."

Henry David Thoreau
- "Men are born to succeed."

Jim Rohn
- "If you don't like how things are change it! You're not a tree."

- "We can have more than we've got because we can become more than we are."

- "I used to say, 'I sure hope things will change'. Then I learned that the only way things are going to change for me is when I change."

- "If you are not financially independent by the time you are forty or fifty, it doesn't mean that you are living in the wrong country or at the wrong time. It simply means that you have the wrong plan."

John Wooden
- "We're not all equal as far as intelligence is concerned. We're not equal as far as size. We're not all equal as far as appearance. We do not all have the same opportunities. We're not born in the same environments, but we're all absolutely equal in having the opportunity to make the most of what we have and not comparing or worrying about what others have."

THE SUCCESS FORMULA FOR PERSONAL GROWTH

Pat Croce
- "If you don't like what you're getting, then change what you're doing. It's up to you."

Robert Kiyosaki
- "It's not what you have to 'do' that needs to change. It's first how you 'think' that needs to change. It's who you have to 'be' in order to 'do' what needs to be done.

  The good news is that it doesn't cost much money to change your thinking. In fact, it can be done for free."

Steven Covey
- "There are three constants in life... change, choice and principles."

- "Every human has four endowments- self awareness, conscience, independent will and creative imagination. These give us the ultimate human freedom... The power to choose, to respond, to change."

Thomas Edison
- "If we did all the things we are capable of, we would literally astound ourselves."

Tony Robbins
- "We can change our lives. We can do, have, and be exactly what we wish."

- "We all have within our grasp the ability to profoundly transform our lives if only we are willing to make clear decisions and take dramatic action to follow through on them."

- "Your current situation does not determine your future. Your future is determined by your decision to succeed."

- "Using the power of decision gives you the capacity to get past any excuse to change any and every part of your life in an instant."

Regardless Of Past Or Present Circumstances You Can Set A Better Direction And Overcome Your Past Or Present.

YOU HAVE THE POWER TO CHANGE AND IMPROVE YOUR LIFE

Buddha
"No matter how hard the past, you can always begin again."

Brian Tracy
"It doesn't matter where you are coming from. All that matters is where you are going."

Carl Bard
"Though no one can go back and make a brand new start, anyone can start from now and make a brand new ending."

David J. Schwartz
"The important thing is not where you were or where you are but where you want to go."

"It isn't what one has that's important. Rather, it's how much one is planning to get that counts."

George Matthew Adams
"It is no disgrace to start all over. It is usually an opportunity."

George Eliot
"It is never too late to be what you might have been."

Henry Ford
"There isn't a person anywhere who isn't capable of doing more than he thinks he can."

Nido Qubein
"Your present circumstances don't determine where you can go; they merely determine where you start."

Oliver Wendall Holmes, Jr.
"The great thing in this world is not so much where we stand as in what direction we are moving."

Pope John XXIII
"Consult not your fears but your hopes and your dreams. Think not about your frustrations, but about your unfulfilled potential. Concern yourself not with what you tried and failed in, but with what it is still possible for you to do."

THE SUCCESS FORMULA FOR PERSONAL GROWTH

Robert Louis Stevenson
- "Everyone who got where he is has had to begin where he was."

Steven Covey
- "Live out of your imagination, not your history."

Tony Robbins
- "It's not what's happening to you now or what has happened in your past that determines who you become. Rather, it's your decisions about what to focus on, what things mean to you, and what you're going to do about them that will determine your ultimate destiny."

W. Clement Stone
- "Regardless of who you are or what you have been, you can be what you want to be."

Wayne Dyer
- "With everything that has happened to you, you can either feel sorry for yourself or treat what has happened as a gift. Everything is either an opportunity to grow or an obstacle to keep you from growing. You get to choose."

Zig Ziglar
- "If you don't like who you are and where you are, don't worry about it because you're not stuck either with who you are or where you are. You can grow. You can change. You can be more than you are."

YOU HAVE THE POWER TO CHANGE AND IMPROVE YOUR LIFE

A Little Change Can Make a Big Difference.

Jim Rohn
- "You don't have to change that much for it to make a great deal of difference. A few simple disciplines can have a major impact on how your life works out in the next 90 days, let alone in the next 12 months or the next 3 years."

You Are Never Too Old To Change And Improve.

C.S. Lewis
- "You are never too old to set another goal or to dream a new dream."

Mark Twain
- "Age is an issue of mind over matter. If you don't mind, it doesn't matter."

Pablo Picasso
- "Youth has no age."

6

Create The Life You Want To Live And Have Remembered

Jerry's Tips:

- If you only had one minute left to live would you be content with what you have accomplished in life?

- If you only had six months to live what would you spend the last six months of your life doing?

- Live your life to the fullest so you will have no regrets of wishing you failed to try to do or accomplish something.

- If you want to be well remembered when you are gone, lead a memorable life.

- Commit to yourself right now that you will lead your life so that you will have no regrets and that it will be memorable.

Bruce Lee
- "The key to immortality is first living a life worth remembering."

Epictetus
- "First say to yourself what you would be; and then do what you have to do."

Jackie Robinson
- "A life is not important except in the impact it has on other lives."

Jim Rohn
- "We all suffer from one of the two pains: the pain of discipline or the pain of regret. The difference is discipline weighs ounces while regret weighs tons."

CREATE THE LIFE YOU WANT TO LIVE AND HAVE REMEMBERED

Leonardo da Vinci
- "As a well-spent day brings happy sleep, so a life well spent brings happy death."

Mark Twain
- "Twenty years from now you will be more disappointed by the things that you didn't do than by the ones you did do. So throw off the bowlines. Sail away from the safe harbor. Catch the trade winds in your sails. Explore. Dream. Discover."

Pat Croce
- "Your Obituary.
  How do you think you'd feel if you could read your own obituary? Would it say what you want it to say?
  Would it reflect how you want to be remembered?"

Roger Smith
- "You don't just stumble into your future. You create your own future."

Socrates
- "The nearest way to glory is to strive to be what you wish to be thought to be."

Steven Covey
- "Begin with the end in mind."

- "How different our lives are when we really know what is deeply important to us, and keeping that picture in mind, we manage ourselves each day to be and to do what really matters most."

Steve Jobs
- "When I was 17, I read a quote that went something like: 'If you live each day as if it was your last, someday you'll most certainly be right.' It made an impression on me, and since then, for the past 33 years, I have looked in the mirror every morning and asked myself: 'If today were the last day of my life, would I want to do what I am about to do today?' And whenever the answer has been 'No' for too many days in a row, I know I need to change something."

THE SUCCESS FORMULA FOR PERSONAL GROWTH

- "Remembering that I'll be dead soon is the most important tool I've ever encountered to help me make the big choices in life. Because almost everything – all external expectations, all pride, all fear of embarrassment or failure – these things just fall away in the face of death, leaving only what is truly important. Remembering that you are going to die is the best way I know to avoid the trap of thinking you have something to lose. You are already naked. There is no reason not to follow your heart."

- "Your time is limited, so don't waste it living someone else's life. Don't be trapped by dogma – which is living with the results of other people's thinking. Don't let the noise of other's opinions drown out your own inner voice. And most important, have the courage to follow your heart and intuition. They somehow already know what you truly want to become. Everything else is secondary."

7

Different Results Require A Different Approach

Jerry's Tips:

- If what you are doing is not working to make you successful, you must do something different.

- If you keep doing the same thing, it's silly to expect you'll get a different result.

- To have something different and more than you have now, you have to 'do different' and 'become more.'

- What you do in life and 99.9% of what happens to you in life is a direct result of what you feel, think, say, and do. To improve your life you must feel, think, say or do something different than you are now.

Albert Einstein
- "Insanity is doing the same things over and over and expecting different results."

- "We can't solve problems by using the same kind of thinking we used when we created them."

Jim Rohn
- "Unless you change how you are, you'll always have what you've got."

Les Brown
- "You cannot expect to achieve new goals or move beyond your present circumstances unless you change."

Oprah Winfrey
- "We can't become what we need to be by remaining what we are."

THE SUCCESS FORMULA FOR PERSONAL GROWTH

Pat Croce
- "If you want different you have to think and act different."

Tony Robbins
- "If you do what you've always done, you'll get what you've always gotten."

8

Take Responsibility For Your Life

Jerry's Tips:

- No one is responsible for your life and success except you.

- To accomplish anything in life you must take responsibility for your own life, decide what you want to do, and then do it.

- Be accountable to yourself. Are you moving closer to or further away from success?

- It's your life. If you want it to turn out right, take responsibility for it and make it the life you truly want and deserve.

- Stop wallowing in your self-pity and feeling sorry for your current circumstances. It's a waste of time and won't get you anywhere. Take responsibility for yourself and 'do' something to change and improve your life.

- Be responsible for yourself and those you are responsible for!

- Never settle for ordinary. You must always feel that you are extraordinary.

- Stop avoiding reality and begin to consciously live your life.

- There have always been successful people, you just need to decide that you want to be one and plan for it.

- If you sit around all day and do nothing to significantly advance your future your spirit will rust out and you'll live at best an average or mediocre life.

- Take conscious control over your life.

THE SUCCESS FORMULA FOR PERSONAL GROWTH

- Declare to yourself 'right now' that you can and will improve your life!

- Win or lose, only you hold the key to your own destiny, and you must put it in the lock and turn it to open the door to your success.

Abraham Lincoln
- "Always bear in mind that your own resolution to succeed is more important than any other one thing."

Amelia Earhart
- "Some of us have great runways already built for us. If you have one, take off! But if you don't have one, realize it is your responsibility to grab a shovel and build one for yourself and for those who will follow after you."

Anonymous
- "The best time to start thinking about your retirement is before the boss does."

- "Your future depends on many things, but mostly on you."

- "God gave us two ends. One to sit on and one to think with. Success depends on which one you use; heads you win -- tails, you lose."

- "You lose out on 100% of the opportunities that you never go for."

- "Nothing ventured -- Nothing gained."

- "It is not what life hands us, but what we do about it."

Benjamin Disraeli
- "Circumstances are beyond human control, but our conduct is in our own power."

Benjamin Franklin
- "God helps those who help themselves."

- "How few there are who have courage enough to own their faults, or resolution enough to mend them."

TAKE RESPONSIBILITY FOR YOUR LIFE

Billie Jean King
- "Champions take responsibility. When the ball is coming over the net, you can be sure I want the ball."

Bob Moawad
- "The best day of your life is the one on which you decide your life is your own. No apologies or excuses. No one to lean on, rely on, or blame. The gift is yours - it is an amazing journey - and you alone are responsible for the quality of it. This is the day your life really begins."

- "You can't leave footprints in the sands of time if you're sitting on your butt. And who wants to leave butt prints in the sands of time."

Brian Tracy
- "The biggest mistake we could ever make in our lives is to think we work for anybody but ourselves."

- "I found every single successful person I've ever spoken to had a turning point. The turning point was when they made a clear, specific unequivocal decision that they were not going to live like this anymore; they were going to achieve success. Some people make that decision at 15 and some people make it at 50, and most people never make it all."

- "Those who don't set goals for themselves are forever doomed to work to achieve the goals of others."

Carol Burnett
- "Only I can change my life. No one can do it for me."

Christopher Reeve
- "So many of our dreams at first seem impossible, then they seem improbable, and then, when we summon the will, they soon become inevitable."

Confucius
- "If you shoot for the stars and hit the moon, it's OK. But you've got to shoot for something. A lot of people don't even shoot."

David Viscott
- "In the end, the only people who fail are those who do not try."

THE SUCCESS FORMULA FOR PERSONAL GROWTH

Denis Waitley
- "There are two primary choices in life: to accept conditions as they exist, or accept the responsibility for changing them."

- "The winners in life think constantly in terms of I can, I will, and I am. Losers, on the other hand, concentrate their waking thoughts on what they should have or would have done, or what they can't do."

Earl Nightingale
- "The biggest mistake that you can make is to believe that you are working for somebody else. Job security is gone. The driving force of a career must come from the individual. Remember: Jobs are owned by the company, you own your career!"

- "We can let circumstances rule us, or we can take charge and rule our lives from within."

- "We all walk in the dark and each of us must learn to turn on his or her own light."

Gene Roddenberry
- "A man either lives life as it happens to him, meets it head-on and licks it, or he turns his back on it and starts to wither away."

Jack Canfield
- "The real truth is that there is only one person responsible for the quality of the life you live. That person is YOU."

Jack Welch
- "Control your own destiny or someone else will."

Jackie Robinson
- "Life is not a spectator sport. If you're going to spend your whole life in the grandstand just watching what goes on, in my opinion you're wasting your life."

Jim Rohn
- "If you don't design your own life plan, chances are you'll fall into someone else's plan. And guess what they have planned for you? Not much."

Take Responsibility for Your Life

- "You must take personal responsibility. You cannot change the circumstances, the seasons, or the wind, but you can change yourself. That is something you have charge of."

- "You can't hire someone else to do your push-ups for you."

- "The worst thing one can do is not to try, to be aware of what one wants and not give in to it, to spend years in silent hurt wondering if something could have materialized - never knowing."

Lao Tzu
- "The journey of a thousand miles begins with a single step."

Les Brown
- "Accept responsibility for your life. Know that it is you who will get you where you want to go, no one else."

- "If you take responsibility for yourself you will develop a hunger to accomplish your dreams."

- "No one will take better care of your dream than you."

- "Life is a fight for territory and once you stop fighting for what you want, what you don't want will automatically take over."

Louis E. Boone
- "The saddest summary of a life contains three descriptions: could have, might have and should have."

Madonna
- "Better to live one year as a tiger, than a hundred as a sheep."

Mark Twain
- "Don't go around saying the world owes you a living. The world owes you nothing. It was here first."

Mickey Rooney
- "Someone once asked me what I want on my epitaph when I pass away. Just the words – 'I tried.' That's what this game of life is all about. Trying. There's the tryers, the criers, and the liars."

Napoleon Bonaparte
- "Circumstances—what are circumstances? I make circumstances."

THE SUCCESS FORMULA FOR PERSONAL GROWTH

Napoleon Hill
- "You might well remember that nothing can bring you success but yourself."

- "It takes half your life before you discover life is a do-it-yourself project."

Neal Boortz
- "The key to accepting responsibility for your life is to accept the fact that your choices, every one of them, are leading you inexorably to either success or failure, however you define those terms."

Nora Roberts
- "If you don't go after what you want, you'll never have it. If you don't ask, the answer is always no. If you don't step forward, you're always in the same place."

Og Mandino
- "It's all up to you. No one else can live your life for you. No one else can succeed for you! It's your move."

Roger Von Oech
- "Either you let your life slip away by not doing the things you want to do, or you get up and do them."

Pat Croce
- "Don't live as a prisoner of the past. Enjoy the freedom of today and step through the cell door toward your future."

Oprah Winfrey
- "It doesn't matter who you are, where you come from. The ability to triumph begins with you. Always."

Russell Simmons
- "In the end, the overriding factor in whether or not you realize your dreams is going to be you. Not the world. YOU."

Samuel Smiles
- "Life will always be to a large extent what we ourselves make it."

- "Much will be done if we do but try. Nobody knows what he can do till he has tried; and few try their best till they have been forced to do it."

Take Responsibility for Your Life

Seneca
- "It is not because things are difficult that we do not dare; it is because we do not dare that things are difficult."

Tony Robbins
- "Whatever happens, take responsibility."

Voltaire
- "Each player must accept the cards life deals him or her. But once they are in hand, he or she alone must decide how to play the cards in order to win the game."

Wayne Gretzky
- "You miss 100% of the shots you never take."

William H. Johnson
- "If it is to be, it is up to me."

William Shakespeare
- "This above all; to thine own self be true."

Zig Ziglar
- "You cannot solve a problem until you acknowledge that you have one and accept responsibility for solving it."

9

Don't Make Excuses, Complain, Or Blame Anyone Or Anything For Your Present Circumstances

Jerry's Tips:

- Don't make excuses, whine, complain, or blame anyone.

- You can't excuse your way to accomplish anything. Only doing something produces results.

- When you make an excuse you reduce your self-esteem and confidence. By admitting to your mistakes you increase your power to take responsibility for your life and make it a success.

- When you are supposed to do something and you don't accomplish it because something 'out of your control' prevented it that's a logical 'reason' why you couldn't get it done.

    But if you didn't do it because you decided to do something else instead that you preferred to do, or didn't try hard enough, or you attempt to shift the blame to someone who is not actually at fault, and you are asking to be relieved of your 'personal responsibility' for not having done what you were supposed to do – that's an 'excuse!'.

- An excuse is your irresponsible attempt to shift blame or accountability from yourself to someone or something else for something that otherwise would be considered your personal responsibility for happening or not happening depending upon the circumstances.

DON'T MAKE EXCUSES, COMPLAIN OR BLAME ANYONE OR ANYTHING FOR YOUR PRESENT CIRCUMSTANCES

Don't Make Excuses.

Anonymous
- "You can make things happen, or you can make excuses; but you cannot do both at the same time."

- "Losers find excuses, winners find solutions."

Benjamin Franklin
- "He that is good for making excuses is seldom good for anything else."

Catherine Pulsifer
- "Sometimes, people use age as a convenient excuse. 'I'm too old to start something new', or, 'I couldn't learn that at my age.' Other people, though, go on to achieve their greatest accomplishments in life in later years."

David J. Schwartz
- "It is no use. I am too old (or too Young).
This excuse has closed the door of real opportunity to thousands of individuals. They think their age is wrong, so they don't even bother to try. When you beat down your fears of age limitations, you add years to your life as well as success.

   Solution: Look at your present age positively. Think I am still young and not I am already old. Compute how much productive time you have left. Invest future time in doing what you really want to do. I am going to start now; my best years are ahead of me."

Earl Nightingale
- "Don't let the fear of the time it will take to accomplish something stand in the way of your doing it. The time will pass anyway; we might just as well put that passing time to the best possible use."

Florence Nightingale
- "I attribute my success to this - I never gave or took any excuse."

General George S. Patton
- "Do not make excuses, whether it's your fault or not."

George Washington Carver
- "Ninety-nine percent of the failures come from people who have the habit of making excuses."

J. Michael Straczynski
- "People spend too much time finding other people to blame, too much energy finding excuses for not being what they are capable of being, and not enough energy putting themselves on the line, growing out of the past, and getting on with their lives."

Napoleon Hill
- "The best job goes to the person who can get it done without passing the buck or coming back with excuses."

Rudyard Kipling
- "We have forty million reasons for failure, but not a single excuse."

Sam Silverstein
- "An excuse is a lie that we tell ourselves to sell ourselves and try to sell to others. And until we stand up and say no more excuses our greatest success will evade us. We need to take personal responsibility when things go wrong."

Thomas Fuller
- "Bad excuses are worse than none."

Don't Complain Or Blame Anyone Or Anything For Your Present Circumstances.

Benjamin Franklin
- "Any fool can criticize, condemn and complain and most fools do."

David J. Schwartz
- "Lot's of folks go through life explaining their mediocrity with 'hard luck,' 'tough luck,' 'bad luck.' These people are still like children, immature, searching for sympathy. Without realizing it, they fail to see opportunities to grow bigger, stronger, more self-reliant."

- "Stop blaming luck. Blaming luck never got anyone where they wanted to go."

DON'T MAKE EXCUSES, COMPLAIN OR BLAME ANYONE OR ANYTHING FOR YOUR PRESENT CIRCUMSTANCES

George Bernard Shaw
- "People are always blaming their circumstances for what they are. I don't believe in circumstances. The people who get on in this world are the people who get up and look for the circumstances they want, and, if they can't find them, make them."

James Allen
- "The very fact that you are a complainer, shows that you deserve your lot."

- "If you spend five minutes complaining, you just wasted five minutes. If you continue complaining, it won't be long before they haul you out to a financial desert and there let you choke on the dust of your own regret."

John Wooden
- "Don't Whine, Don't Complain, Don't Alebi."

10

Your Choices Have Consequences

Jerry's Tips:

- You have the power to choose what you do and that gives you the power to control your life and to make it a success or a failure.

- Every choice you make has consequences.

- You have the choice to control and improve your life or to just drift along.

- If you don't make conscious decisions and choose to guide your life it will always feel out-of-control.

- Your life up until today is the result of all of your past choices. You can choose now to act to improve your life today and in future.

- It's your choice to live up or down to your expectations.

- Frequently people don't realize they have a choice to do or not do something. Look out for choices you can make to improve your life.

- Ask anyone and they will say they want to have a happy, successful and fulfilled life. But, you can't get there by words alone. You must choose to do something to create that life for yourself – and then go out and do it.

- Choose right now that you will invest your time to improve your life!

Your Choices Have Consequences

Alfred A. Montapert
"Nobody ever did, or ever will, escape the consequences of his choices."

Aristotle
"For what is the best choice, for each individual it is the highest it is possible for him to achieve."

Catherine Pulsifer
"We all find ourselves in situations that at times seem hopeless. And, we all have the choice to do nothing or take action."

David J. Schwartz
"A good idea if not acted upon produces terrible psychological pain. But a good idea acted upon brings enormous mental satisfaction. Got a good idea? Then do something about it."

Deepak Chopra
"Whether you like it or not, everything that is happening at this moment is a result of the choices you've made in the past."

Elizabeth Kubler-Ross
"I believe that we are solely responsible for our choices, and we have to accept the consequences of every deed, word, and thought throughout our lifetime."

James Allen
"Man is made or unmade by himself. By the right choice he ascends. As a being of power, intelligence, and love, and the lord of his own thoughts, he holds the key to every situation."

Jim Rohn
"When you are tough on yourself, life is going to be infinitely easier on you."

Jean Nidetch
"It's choice--not chance--that determines your destiny."

J. K. Rowling
"It is our choices that show what we truly are, far more than our abilities."

THE SUCCESS FORMULA FOR PERSONAL GROWTH

Jim Collins
"Greatness is not a function of circumstance. Greatness, it turns out, is largely a matter of conscious choice, and discipline."

Joan Baez
"You don't get to choose how you're going to die. Or when. You can only decide how you're going to live. Now."

John C. Maxwell
"We choose what attitudes we have right now. And it's a continuing choice."

Og Mandino
"I have a choice and I will not let my life be fed to swine nor will I let it be ground under the rocks of failure and despair to be broken open and devoured by the will of others."

Oprah Winfrey
"Understand that the right to choose your own path is a sacred privilege. Use it. Dwell in possibility."

Pat Croce
"You can choose to do anything in life that you want as long as you are willing to accept the consequences of your choices."

"No one can make you do anything. It's your choice. Do the thing or accept the consequences of not doing the thing."

"There's a choice you have to make in everything you do."

"Always keep in mind, the choice you make, makes you."

"It's not your conditions, but rather your decisions that determine your destiny."

"Destiny isn't by chance. It's by choice."

Pat Riley
"Look for your choices, pick the best one, then go with it."

Your Choices Have Consequences

Richard Back
- "All we see of someone at any moment is a snapshot of their life, there in riches or poverty, in joy or despair. Snapshots don't show the million decisions that led to that moment."

Shakti Gawain
- "I like to think of myself as an artist, and my life is my greatest work of art. Every moment is a moment of creation, and each moment of creation contains infinite possibilities. I can do things the way I've always done them, or I can look at all the different alternatives, and try something new and different and potentially more rewarding. Every moment presents a new opportunity and a new decision. What a wonderful game we are all playing, and what a magnificent art form...."

Steven Covey
- "While we are free to choose our actions, we are not free to choose the consequences of our actions."

- "Between stimulus and response is our greatest power - the freedom to choose."

- "Between stimulus and response there is a space. In that space lies our freedom and power to choose our response. In those choices lie our growth and our happiness."

- "Until a person can say deeply and honestly, 'I am what I am today because of the choices I made yesterday,' that person cannot say, 'I choose otherwise'."

Tony Robbins
- "It is in your moments of decision that your destiny is shaped."

- "The 3 decisions that control your destiny:
  1. Your decisions about what to focus on,
  2. Your decisions about what things mean to you,
  3. Your decisions about what to do to create the results you desire."

Wayne Dyer
- "Be miserable. Or motivate yourself. Whatever has to be done, it's always your choice."

THE SUCCESS FORMULA FOR PERSONAL GROWTH

W. Clement Stone
- "You always do what you want to do. This is true with every act. You may say that you had to do something, or that you were forced to, but actually, whatever you do, you do by choice. Only you have the power to choose for yourself."

Zig Ziglar
- "Every choice you make has an end result."

11

Your Good And Bad Habits Can Lead To Or Prevent Success, Happiness And Fulfillment

Jerry's Tips:

- A habit is something you do regularly and consistently that satisfies a need such as brushing your teeth after every meal, reading a book every week to learn something new, or drinking whiskey every day.

- What you do habitually determines whether you will become successful, be ordinary, or be a failure.

- Good habits lead you to success.

- Bad habits lead you away from success.

- Successful people have the habit of setting goals and taking relentless action to achieve their goals. Not setting goals and working hard to achieve them is also a habit.

- It's extremely difficult to try to stop doing a bad habit because you will be left with the unsatisfied need that the bad habit fulfilled and the bad habit will eventually return to satisfy it. What you need to do is figure out how to replace your bad habit with a good habit that satisfies the same need.

Aristotle
- "We are what we repeatedly do. Excellence, therefore, is not an act, but a habit."

Benjamin Franklin
- "Your net worth to the world is usually determined by what remains after your bad habits are subtracted from your good ones."

THE SUCCESS FORMULA FOR PERSONAL GROWTH

Brian Tracy
- "Successful people are simply those with successful habits."

- "The key to success is for you to make a habit throughout your life of doing the things you fear."

Dale Carnegie
- "Feeling sorry for yourself, and your present condition, is not only a waste of energy but the worst habit you could possibly have."

General Colin Powell
- "If you are going to achieve excellence in big things, you develop the habit in little matters. Excellence is not an exception, it is a prevailing attitude."

Horace Mann
- "Habit is a cable; we weave a thread of it each day, and at last we cannot break it."

Jim Rohn
- "Motivation is what gets you started. Habit is what keeps you going."

- "Failure is not a single, cataclysmic event. You don't fail overnight. Instead, failure is a few errors in judgment, repeated everyday."

John Dryden
- "We first make our habits, and then our habits make us."

Og Mandino
- "The only difference between those who have failed and those who have succeeded lies in the difference of their habits. Good habits are the key to all success. Bad habits are the unlocked door to failure."

- "The victory of success is half won when one gains the habit of setting goals and achieving them. Even the most tedious chore will become endurable as you parade through each day convinced that every task, no matter how menial or boring, brings you closer to achieving your dreams."

Samuel Johnson
- "The chains of habit are generally too small to be felt until they are too strong to be broken."

YOUR GOOD AND BAD HABITS CAN LEAD TO OR PREVENT SUCCESS, HAPPINESS AND FULFILLMENT

Tony Robbins

- "For changes to be of any true value, they've got to be lasting and consistent. Any time you sincerely want to make a change, the first thing you must do is to raise your standards. When people ask me what really changed my life eight years ago, I tell them that absolutely the most important thing was changing what I demanded of myself. I wrote down all the things I would no longer accept in my life, all the things I would no longer tolerate, and all the things that I aspired to becoming."

- "In essence, if we want to direct our lives, we must take control of our consistent actions. It's not what we do once in a while that shapes our lives, but what we do consistently."

Vince Lombardi

- "Winning is not a sometime thing: it's an all the time thing. You don't win once in a while; you don't do the right thing once in a while; you do them right all the time. Winning is a habit. Unfortunately, so is losing."

- "Once you learn to quit, it becomes a habit."

Zig Ziglar

- "Motivation gets you going but habit gets you there."

12

You Become What You Think About Most Of The Time

Jerry's Tips:

- Everything you do begins with a thought.

- Everything in our world was created by a thought; radio, TV, computers, the Internet, clothes, cars, music, medicine, etc.

- We become and attract what we think about most of the time.

- Your past thoughts have brought you to where you are today; your present and future thoughts will take you to where you go tomorrow.

- Your ability to focus and control your own thoughts will enable you to plan and achieve your goals.

- We have no limitations except those that we place in our own minds.

- Good thoughts produce good action, bad thoughts produce bad action.

- Positive thoughts lead to positive results, negative thoughts lead to negative results.

- If you change your thoughts, you will change your life. It's as simple as that.

- Think big thoughts to make big changes and big improvements in your life.

You Become What You Think About Most of the Time

Benjamin Disraeli
- "Nurture your mind with great thoughts, for you will never go any higher than you think."

Blaise Pascal
- "Man's greatness lies in his power of thought."

Bruce Lee
- "As you think, so shall you become."

Buddha
- "We are what we think."

- "The mind is everything. What you think you become."

- "All that we are is the result of what we have thought."

David J. Schwartz
- "How you think determines how you act. How you act in turn determines how others react to you."

- "Capacity is a state of mind. How much we can do depends upon how much we think we can do. When you really believe you can do more, your mind thinks creatively and shows you the way."

Donald Trump
- "As long as you're going to be thinking anyway, THINK BIG."

Earl Nightingale
- "Your world is a living expression of how you are using and have used your mind."

- "Throughout all history, the great wise men and teachers, philosophers, and prophets have disagreed with one another on many different things. It is only on this one point that they are in complete and unanimous agreement. - We become what we think about."

- "Everything begins with an idea."

- "The mind moves in the direction of our currently dominant thoughts."

- "The more intensely we feel about an idea or a goal, the more assuredly the idea, buried deep in our subconscious, will direct us along the path to its fulfillment."

- "Believe and succeed."

- "He who thinks about nothing becomes nothing."

- "A person who is thinking about a concrete and worthwhile goal is going to reach it, because that's what he's thinking about. Conversely, the person who has no goal, who doesn't know where he's going, and whose thoughts must therefore be thoughts of confusion, anxiety, fear, and worry will thereby create a life of frustration, fear, anxiety and worry."

George Matthew Adams
- "What you think means more than anything else in your life. More than what you earn, more than where you live, more than your social position, and more than what anyone else may think about you."

Henry Ford
- "If you think you CAN do a thing, or think you CAN'T do a thing, you're RIGHT!"

James Allen
- "Good thoughts bear good fruit, bad thoughts bear bad fruit."

- "You are today where your thoughts have brought you; you will be tomorrow where your thoughts take you."

- "You cannot escape the results of your thoughts. Whatever your present environment may be, you will fall, remain or rise with your thoughts, your vision, and your ideal. You will become as small as your controlling desire; as great as your dominant aspiration."

- "A man is literally what he thinks."

- "All that you accomplish or fail to accomplish with your life is the direct result of your thoughts."

- "All that a man achieves and all that he fails to achieve is the direct result of his own thoughts."

You Become What You Think About Most of the Time

Jesus Christ
- "As a man thinketh in his heart, so is he."

John C. Maxwell
- "Successful people have their behavior (thinking & actions) affect their feelings. Unsuccessful people allow their feelings to affect their behavior."

Marcus Aurelius
- "A man's life is what his thoughts make of it."

- "The happiness of your life depends upon the quality of your thoughts, therefore guard accordingly; and take care that you entertain no notions unsuitable to virtue, and reasonable nature."

- "In the morning, when you are sluggish about getting up, let this thought be present: 'I am rising to a man's work.' "

Mother Teresa
- "The first step to becoming is to will it."

Napoleon Hill
- "What the mind of man can conceive and believe, it can achieve."

- "We have no limitations except those that we place in our own minds."

- "Man, alone, has the power to transform his thoughts into physical reality; man, alone, can dream and make his dreams come true."

- "Desire is the starting point of all achievement, not a hope, not a wish, but a keen pulsating desire which transcends everything."

Norman Vincent Peale
- "If you think in negative terms, you will get negative results."

- "If you think in positive terms, you will achieve positive results."

- "Believe that you are defeated, believe it long enough, and it is likely to become a fact."

Oprah Winfrey
- "I know for sure that what we dwell on is who we become."

THE SUCCESS FORMULA FOR PERSONAL GROWTH

Publilius Syrus
- "A wise man will be master of his mind. A fool will be its slave."

Ralph Waldo Emerson
- "We become what we think about all day long."

- "The ancestor of every action is a thought."

Dr. Robert H. Schuller
- "You are what you think about all day long."

W. Clement Stone
- "All personal achievement starts in the mind of the individual. Your personal achievement starts in your mind."

Wayne Dyer
- "As you think so shall you be!"

- "Behind every thought is an energy."

Willis Harman
- "Perhaps the only limits to the human mind are those we believe in."

13

Believe It's Possible
You Can Accomplish Your Dreams!

Jerry's Tips:

- Beliefs are what we think are possible.

- Always think that your goals are possible. Believe you can accomplish them.

- Never think or say 'I can't do or have something' that you want to do or have. Instead, think and say 'I can' and figure out 'how' to do or have it.

- Your beliefs are effected by how you interpret the world around you.

- Believe that the world is a good place and that good things will happen to you if you make the most of yourself – and they will.

- Events in your life only have the meaning you attach to them. Don't attach negative meaning to events. Just learn from them and move forward.

- Do not allow yourself to believe that you might fail at something. If you believe you might fail at something you plant the seed of failure which grows very quickly.

- To truly believe you can do something it's not enough to just say the words in your mind or out loud that you believe it. You must pack emotional content into your beliefs for them to be accepted by your mind and affect your actions. Learn to feel your beliefs not just know them."

- You can accomplish anything within your ability if you believe with all your heart and mind that you can.

THE SUCCESS FORMULA FOR PERSONAL GROWTH

Bob Proctor
- "The only limits in our life are those we impose on ourselves."

Bruce Lee
- "When you say that something is impossible, you have made it impossible."

- "We need emotional content in all of our actions to execute them to their fullest."

Charles F. Kettering
- "Believe and act as if it were impossible to fail."

- "Our imagination is the only limit to what we can hope to have in the future."

David Blaine
- "We are all capable of infinitely more than we believe. In truth, the only restrictions on our capacity to astonish ourselves and each other are imposed by our own minds."

David J. Schwartz
- "Belief is the thermostat that regulates what we accomplish in life."

- "Believe it can be done. When you believe something can be done, really believe, your mind will find the ways to do it. Believing a solution paves the way to solution."

- "Belief works this way: Belief, the I'm-positive-I-can attitude, generates the power, skill, and energy needed to do. When you believe I-can-do-it, the how-to-do-it develops."

- "When you believe, your mind finds ways to do."

- "When you believe something is impossible, your mind goes to work for you to prove why. But when you believe, really believe, something can be done, your mind goes to work for you and helps you find the ways to do it."

- "The 'Okay-I'll-give-it-a-try-but-I-don't-think-it-will-work' attitude produces failures."

BELIEVE IT'S POSSIBLE YOU CAN ACCOMPLISH YOUR DREAMS!

George Lucas
[Obi-Wan Kenobi to Luke Skywalker in Star Wars]
- "Many of the truths we cling to depend greatly on our point of view."

J. K. Rowling
- "Anything's possible if you've got enough nerve."

James Allen
- "Men often become what they believe themselves to be. If I believe I cannot do something, it makes me incapable of doing it. But when I believe I can, then I acquire the ability to do it even if I didn't have it in the beginning."

- "The outer conditions of a person's life will always be found to reflect their inner beliefs."

Jim Rohn
- "The greatest change to go from average to fortune is not so much an increase in knowledge, but rather, a change in our emotions about achieving our goals."

Lance Armstrong
- "Anything's possible. You can be told you have a 90% chance or a 50% chance or a 1% chance, but you have to believe, and you have to fight."

Martin Luther King, Jr.
- "Take the first step in faith. You don't have to see the whole staircase. Just take the first step."

Napoleon Hill
- "No one is ready for a thing until he believes he can acquire it. The state of mind must be belief, not mere hope or wish."

- "There are no limitations to the mind except those we acknowledge."

- "The starting point of all achievement is desire. Keep this constantly in mind. Weak desires bring weak results, just as a small amount of fire makes a small amount of heat."

THE SUCCESS FORMULA FOR PERSONAL GROWTH

Og Mandino
- "Free yourself of the chains stamped 'I can't!' and you will be able to achieve any height you desire. You can do anything ... if you believe you can! Easy? Of course not. Nothing in life worth achieving is easy. Can you pull it off? Yes, but you will never know, unless you try and keep trying."

Richard M. DeVos
- " 'I can.' ... People can do what they believe they can do."

- "The only thing that stands between a man and what he wants from life is often merely the will to try it and the faith to believe that it is possible."

Steven Covey
- "The way we see the problem is the problem."

Tony Robbins
- "Beliefs have the power to create and the power to destroy. Human beings have the awesome ability to take any experience of their lives and create a meaning that disempowers them or one that can literally save their lives."

- "It's not the events of our lives that shape us, but our beliefs as to what those events mean."

- "We are the only beings on the planet who lead such rich internal lives that it's not the events that matter most to us, but rather, it's how we interpret those events that will determine how we think about ourselves and how we will act in the future."

- "You see, it's never the environment; it's never the events of our lives, but the meaning we attach to the events - how we interpret them - that shapes who we are today and who we'll become tomorrow."

- "What we can or cannot do, what we consider possible or impossible, is rarely a function of our true capability. It is more likely a function of our beliefs about who we are."

Whoopi Goldberg
- "I am where I am because I believe in all possibilities."

BELIEVE IT'S POSSIBLE YOU CAN ACCOMPLISH YOUR DREAMS!

William James

- "The greatest discovery of my generation is that human beings can alter their lives by altering their attitudes of mind."

- "We need only in cold blood act as if the thing in question were real, and it will become infallibly real by growing into such a connection with our life that it will become real. It will become so knit with habit and emotion that our interests in it will be those which characterize belief."

- "In almost any subject your passion for the subject will save you. If you only care enough for a result, you will almost certainly attain it. If you wish to be rich, you will be rich; if you wish to be learned, you will be learned; if you wish to be good, you will be good. Only you must, then, really wish these things, and wish them with exclusiveness, and not wish at the same time a hundred other incompatible things just as strongly."

14

Live With Passion, Do What You Love To Do

Jerry's Tips:

- To live your life with passion means to love doing what you do.

- You never get tired or bored doing what you love to do.

- Doing what you love to do is energizing.

- When you do what you love, you are successful.

- When you truly love your work you won't mind the struggle, obstacles and hard work needed to succeed.

- If you search hard enough you will find something that you are or can be very good at and enjoy doing. Doing it will give you a happy, successful and fulfilled life.

- Life is short; don't end up regretting and looking back that you wish you could have spent your life doing what you loved. Figure out what you love to do and find a way to make it a major part of your life. Do it NOW!

Al Duncan
- "One of the keys to greatness is finding a way to do something you love to do, not just something that's 'safe' to do. Many people have experienced a high level of achievement but are stuck in professions they hate. What kind of sense does that make? None. High achievement without fulfillment is a broken way of life."

LIVE WITH PASSION, DO WHAT YOU LOVE TO DO

Anonymous
"If you really want to do something, you'll find a way; if you don't, you'll find an excuse."

Aristotle
"Pleasure in the job puts perfection in the work."

Confucius
"Choose a job you love, and you will never have to work a day in your life."

Chris Evert
"Find something that you're really interested in doing in your life. Pursue it, set goals, and commit yourself to excellence. Do the best you can."

Dale Carnegie
"People rarely succeed unless they enjoy what they are doing."

Donald Trump
"The most important thing in life is to love what you're doing, because that's the only way you'll ever be really good at it."

"Do what you love and you won't work a single day in your life."

"Without passion you don't have energy, without energy you have nothing."

Earl Nightingale
"We are at our very best, and we are happiest, when we are fully engaged in work we enjoy on the journey toward the goal we've established for ourselves. It gives meaning to our time off and comfort to our sleep. It makes everything else in life so wonderful, so worthwhile."

"Get into a line that you will find to be a deep personal interest, something you really enjoy spending twelve to fifteen hours a day working at, and the rest of the time thinking about."

George Burns
"I honestly think it is better to be a failure at something you love than to be a success at something you hate."

THE SUCCESS FORMULA FOR PERSONAL GROWTH

George Lucas
- "You have to find something that you love enough to be able to take risks, jump over the hurdles and break through the brick walls that are always going to be placed in front of you. If you don't have that kind of feeling for what it is you are doing, you'll stop at the first giant hurdle."

Jack Canfield
- "You were born with an inner guidance system that tells you when you are on or off purpose by the amount of joy you are experiencing. The things that bring you the greatest joy are in alignment with your purpose."

- "What you are here to do is what will give you the greatest amount of joy when you are doing it."

Jim Collins
- "The kind of commitment I find among the best performers across virtually every field is a single-minded passion for what they do, an unwavering desire for excellence in the way they think and the way they work. Genuine confidence is what launches you out of bed in the morning, and through your day with a spring in your step."

Jim Rohn
- "The worst days of those who enjoy what they do, are better than the best days of those who don't."

Johnny Carson
- "Never continue in a job you don't enjoy. If you're happy in what you're doing, you'll like yourself, you'll have inner peace. And if you have that, along with physical health, you will have had more success than you could possibly have imagined."

Malcolm S. Forbes
- "The biggest mistake people make in life is not trying to make a living at doing what they most enjoy."

Mia Hamm
- "If you don't love what you do, you won't do it with much conviction or passion."

LIVE WITH PASSION, DO WHAT YOU LOVE TO DO

Napoleon Hill
- "Success in its highest and noblest form calls for peace of mind and enjoyment and happiness which come only to the man who has found the work that he likes best."

Oprah Winfrey
- "Passion is energy. Feel the power that comes from focusing on what excites you."

- "What I know, is that if you do work that you love, and the work fulfills you, the rest will come."

Pat Croce
- "If the love of what you do exceeds the effort of doing it, success is inevitable."

Paul Harvey
- "Like what you do, if you don't like it, do something else."

Steve Jobs
- "You've got to find what you love. And that is as true for your work as it is for your lovers. Your work is going to fill a large part of your life, and the only way to be truly satisfied is to do what you believe is great work. And the only way to do great work is to love what you do. If you haven't found it yet, keep looking. Don't settle. As with all matters of the heart, you'll know when you find it. And, like any great relationship, it just gets better and better as the years roll on. So keep looking until you find it. Don't settle."

- "Sometimes life hits you in the head with a brick. Don't lose faith. I'm convinced that the only thing that kept me going was that I loved what I did."

Thomas Edison
- "I never did a day's work in my life. It was all fun!"

Tiger Woods
- "I get to play golf for a living. What more can you ask for - getting paid for doing what you love."

Tony Robbins
- "Live with passion!"

- "Passion is the genesis of genius."

15

Aspire To Achieve Your Greatest Ambitions And Dreams, Think BIG!

Jerry's Tips:

- You only live once. Why not get the most out of your life?

- You cannot be very successful by looking down or by going after mediocre goals. Look up, higher, and higher still, that is where your dreams and sights should be focused to find success.

- You can't get more out of your life than the amount of your ambition.

- You are put here to live your greatest dreams - not to simply exist.

- Open your mind to big ambition, big dreams and big thoughts.

- If you were not meant to think big you would have been born a fly.

Anna Jameson
- "What we truly and earnestly aspire to be, that in some sense we are. The mere aspiration, by changing the frame of the mind, for the moment realizes itself."

Anonymous
- "The minute you settle for less than you deserve, you get even less than you settled for."

Benjamin Disraeli
- "Life is too short to be little."

Giovanni Niccolini
- "By asking for the impossible we obtain the best possible."

Aspire to Achieve Your Greatest Ambitions and Dreams, Think BIG!

Brian Tracy
- "All successful people men and women are big dreamers. They imagine what their future could be, ideal in every respect, and then they work every day toward their distant vision, that goal or purpose."

Harold Taylor
- "The roots of true achievement lie in the will to become the best that you can become."

Helen Keller
- "I long to accomplish a great and noble task, but it is my chief duty to accomplish small tasks as if they were great and noble."

Henry David Thoreau
- "Go confidently in the direction of your dreams. Live the life you've imagined."

James Allen
- "You will become as small as your controlling desire; as great as your dominant aspiration."

Jim Collins
- "Dreams make you click, juice you, turn you on, excite the living daylights out of you. You cannot wait to get out of bed to continue pursuing your dream. The kind of dream I'm talking about gives meaning to your life. It is the ultimate motivator."

Leo Burnett
- "When you reach for the stars, you may not quite get them, but you won't come up with a handful of mud either."

Marcus Aurelius
- "A man's worth is no greater than the worth of his ambitions."

Michael Harrington
- "It takes a certain level of aspiration before one can take advantage of opportunities that are clearly offered."

Nelson Mandela
- "There is no passion to be found playing small - in settling for a life that is less than the one you are capable of living."

THE SUCCESS FORMULA FOR PERSONAL GROWTH

Norman Vincent Peale
- "I'd rather attempt to do something great and fail, than try doing something ordinary and succeed."

Oscar Wilde
- "To live is the rarest thing in the world. Most people exist, that is all."

Pat Croce
- "Be like a kid and have no ceiling to your dreams."

Ralph Waldo Emerson
- "Without ambition one starts nothing. Without work one finishes nothing. The prize will not be sent to you. You have to win it."

Robert Kiyosaki
- "Big people have big dreams and small people have small dreams. If you want to change who you are, begin by changing the size of your dreams."

Samuel Smiles
- "Man cannot aspire if he looked down; if he rise, he must look up."

Sean (Puff Daddy) Combs
- "I want to convey how beautiful it is to close your eyes and dream. And then to open them and make that dream a reality."

Theodore Roosevelt
- "The credit belongs to the man who spends himself in a worthy cause; who at best knows in the end the triumphs of high achievement; and who at the worst, if he fails, at least fails while daring greatly; so that his place shall never be with those cold and timid souls who know neither defeat nor victory."

Thomas Merton
- "The biggest human temptation is to settle for too little."

Tony Robbins
- "There is no greatness without a passion to be great, whether it's the aspiration of an athlete or an artist, a scientist, a parent, or a businessperson."

- "Most people fail in life because they major in minor things."

ASPIRE TO ACHIEVE YOUR GREATEST AMBITIONS AND DREAMS, THINK BIG!

Walt Disney
- "If you can dream it, you can do it."

William DeMille
- "I have always admired the ability to bite off more than one can chew and then chew it."

16

Your Personal Development Is The Key To Become Happy, Successful And Fulfilled

Jerry's Tips:

- Whether it's called personal development, self-improvement or self-help, the principle is that by spending time to develop and improve yourself to your maximum potential you will be able to achieve success in whatever you want to do.

- Successful athletes, sportsman, business people, entertainers, artists, musicians, parents and students know that the key to their success is to spend time everyday to work on their personal development to improve themselves and reduce their weaknesses.

- Choosing to vigorously and constantly work on their personal development is what separates successful people from people who muddle through life.

- Personal development adds value to your life by giving you the ability to provide service or value to other people's lives.

- Become the best you can be by working on your personal development.

Dr. Phil
- "If you want more, you have to require more from yourself."

James Allen
- "Men are anxious to improve their circumstances, but are unwilling to improve themselves; they therefore remain bound."

YOUR PERSONAL DEVELOPMENT IS THE KEY TO BECOME HAPPY, SUCCESSFUL AND FULFILLED

Jim Rohn

- "Income seldom exceeds personal development."

- "To have more than you've got, become more than you are."

- "Work on your job, you'll make a living, Work on yourself, you'll make a fortune."

- "Formal education will make you a living, self education will make you a fortune."

- "The greatest gift you can give to somebody is your own personal development. I used to say 'if you will take care of me, I will take care of you.' Now I say 'I will take care of me for you, if you will take care of you for me'."

Les Brown

- "You are your most important asset – invest in yourself."

- "All of us are self-made (or self-unmade) but only the successful will admit it."

- "There are winners, there are losers and there are people who have not yet learned how to win."

Ralph Waldo Emerson

- "Make the most of yourself for that's all there is of you."

Samuel Smiles

- "The spirit of self-help is the root of all genuine growth in the individual; and, exhibited in the lives of many, it constitutes the true source of national vigor and strength. Help from without is often enfeebling in its effect, but help from within invariably invigorates."

Tony Robbins

- "Self-Mastery of self comes down to the capacity of an individual to discover what it is that they truly want, what their path is, and then to eliminate the obstacles, which are always internal, that would keep them from being able to fulfill that path on an ongoing basis."

17

Invest Time Every Day To Learn And Improve Yourself

Jerry's Tips:

- There is no greater use of your time than to improve yourself every day in areas that will lead to being successful.

- Deeply believe that you can improve yourself every day and you will find a way.

- Small, constant daily progress will transform you from unskilled, to skilled, to a highly skilled to an expert.

- Always focus on improvement and high standards in everything you think and do.

- Once-a-week ask yourself 'What do I need to know to reach my goals?' Or, 'How can I improve my life?' Or, 'What am I doing wrong?' And then find a way to spend some time each day to learn and improve and take action to do it.

- At the end of each day look back at what you did that day and consider how you could have done it better, or not do certain things that were unproductive and plan how to improve.

- Even if you are now the best in something, unless you aspire to improve, someone will eventually surpass you.

- It is true that 'process' improvement is important. However, at the end of the day processes are performed by people and unless you figure out how to improve the people involved in the process and how they inter-relate you'll only get marginal improvement.

- The more you learn and know the further in life you'll go.

INVEST TIME EVERY DAY TO LEARN AND IMPROVE YOURSELF

- Learn to read faster.

Abraham Lincoln
- "I don't think much of a man who is not wiser today than he was yesterday."

Alexander Graham Bell
- "The most successful men in the end are those whose success is the result of steady accretion... It is the man who carefully advances step by step, with his mind becoming wider and wider - and progressively better able to grasp any theme or situation - persevering in what he knows to be practical, and concentrating his thought upon it, who is bound to succeed in the greatest degree."

Althea Gibson
- "Most of us who aspire to be tops in our fields don't really consider the amount of work required to stay tops."

Arie de Geus
- "Your ability to learn faster than your competition is your only sustainable competitive advantage."

Benjamin Disraeli
- "As a general rule, the most successful man in life is the man who has the best information."

Benjamin Franklin
- "An investment in knowledge pays the best interest."

- "Being ignorant is not so much a shame, as being unwilling to learn."

Bob Proctor
- "It's the little things you do that can make a big difference. What are you attempting to accomplish? What little thing can you do today that will make you more effective? You are probably only one step away from greatness."

Brian Tracy
- "One of the best uses of your time is to increase your competence in your key result areas."

- "Invest the first hour of the day, the 'Golden Hour,' in yourself."

THE SUCCESS FORMULA FOR PERSONAL GROWTH

Bruce Lee
- "If you always put limit on everything you do, physical or anything else. It will spread into your work and into your life. There are no limits. There are only plateaus, and you must not stay there, you must go beyond them."

- "Ever since I was a child I have had this instinctive urge for expansion and growth. To me, the function and duty of a quality human being is the sincere and honest development of one's potential."

- "Using no way as way, having no limitation as limitation."

David J. Schwartz
- "There is endless room for improvement. The successful person doesn't ask, 'Can I do it better?' He knows he can. So he phrases the question: 'how can I do it better?'"

- "The success combination in business is:
    1. Do what you do better (improve the quality of your output), and:
    2. Do more of what you do (increase the quantity of your output)."

Derek Bok
- "If you think education is expensive, try ignorance."

Donald Trump
- "Ask yourself everyday what do I need to know more about?"

- "What can I learn today that I didn't know before?"

- "Finding your purpose may be a lifelong pursuit or you may have discovered it when you were 5 years old. There's no absolute timeline for anyone. That's a good reason never to give up, to keep on discovering things every day."

- "Watch, listen, and learn. You can't know it all yourself. Anyone who thinks they do is destined for mediocrity."

Duke of Wellington
- "Wise people learn when they can. Fools learn when they must."

INVEST TIME EVERY DAY TO LEARN AND IMPROVE YOURSELF

Henry Ford
- "Anyone who stops learning is old, whether at twenty or eighty. Anyone who keeps learning stays young. The greatest thing in life is to keep your mind young."

Jack Welch
- "An organization's ability to learn, and translate that learning into action rapidly, is the ultimate competitive advantage."

Jim Collins
- "How can we do better tomorrow than we did today?"

Jim Rohn
- "Work harder on yourself than you do on your job."
- "My father taught me always to do more than you get paid for as an investment in your future."
- "Motivation alone is not enough. If you have an idiot and you motivate him, now you have a motivated idiot."
- "Don't just read the easy stuff. You may be entertained by it, but you will never grow from it."
- "It isn't what the book costs; it's what it will cost you if you don't read it."
- "The book you don't read, won't help."

Leonardo da Vinci
- "Iron rusts from disuse, stagnant water loses its purity and in cold weather becomes frozen, even so does inaction sap the vigors of the mind."

Les Brown
- "Every morning ask yourself: 'what idea can I think of today that can improve me and enable me to reach my goal?'"

Martina Navratilova
- "The better I get, the more I realize how much better I can get."

THE SUCCESS FORMULA FOR PERSONAL GROWTH

Norman Vincent Peale
- "Empty pockets never held anyone back. Only empty heads and empty hearts can do that."

Og Mandino
- "I am here for a purpose and that purpose is to grow into a mountain, not to shrink to a grain of sand. Henceforth will I apply ALL my efforts to become the highest mountain of all and I will strain my potential until it cries for mercy."

Orison Swett Marden
- "The best educated people are those who are always learning, always absorbing knowledge from every possible source and at every opportunity."

Pat Croce
- "Learning is like working out, hard and painful at times, but definitely worth the effort."

Pat Riley
- "Excellence is the gradual result of always striving to do better."

Russell Simmons
- "You have to be willing to learn new things every day, every second. You can't depend on what you've already been taught."

Francis Bacon
- "Knowledge is power."

Thomas J. Watson
- "Whenever an individual or a business decides that success has been attained, progress stops."

Tony Robbins
- "How am I going to live today in order to create the tomorrow I'm committed to?"

Vince Lombardi
- "Gentlemen, we are going to relentlessly chase perfection, knowing full well we will not catch it, because nothing is perfect. But we are going to relentlessly chase it, because in the process we will catch excellence. I am not remotely interested in just being good."

INVEST TIME EVERY DAY TO LEARN AND IMPROVE YOURSELF

Zen Proverb
"Empty your teacup. You cannot fill a cup that is already full."

18

Practice Self-Control And Self-Discipline To Control Your Thoughts, Emotions And Actions

Jerry's Tips:

- Self-control and self-discipline is training yourself to have the patience to control your conduct by following principles and sound judgment instead of impulses or rash desires to act instantly to seek immediate pleasure.

  It's developing the habit to delay your gratification to see and think through the bigger picture, and do what needs to be done to bring you long lasting success, and not just doing what feels good now or is easy.

- Developing your self-control and self-discipline to habitually set goals, establish priorities, implement long term solutions to problems and not just quick-fixes, and to focus on the things you need to do to accomplish your goals and ignore distracting thoughts and negative emotions is the way to success.

- Develop the self-discipline and self-control to do things correctly when no one is watching you.

Billie Jean King
- "I think self-awareness is probably the most important thing towards being a champion."

Bruce Lee
- "Emotion can be the enemy. If you give in to your emotion, you lose yourself. You must be at one with your emotions because the body always follows the mind."

PRACTICE SELF-CONTROL AND SELF-DISCIPLINE TO CONTROL YOUR THOUGHTS, EMOTIONS AND ACTIONS

Confucius
- "He who conquers himself is the mightiest warrior."

Jim Rohn
- "Discipline is the bridge between goals and accomplishment."

- "The least lack of discipline starts to erode our self-esteem."

- "Discipline is the foundation upon which all success is built. Lack of discipline inevitably leads to failure."

Lao Tzu
- "He who controls others may be powerful, but he who has mastered himself is mightier still."

M. Scott Peck
- "Delaying gratification is a process of scheduling the pain and pleasure of life in such a way as to enhance the pleasure by meeting and experiencing the pain first and getting it over with."

Margaret Thatcher
- "Disciplining yourself to do what you know is right and importance, although difficult, is the highroad to pride, self-esteem, and personal satisfaction."

Napoleon Hill
- "Self-disciplined begins with the mastery of your thoughts. If you don't control what you think, you can't control what you do. Simply, self-discipline enables you to think first and act afterward."

Norman Vincent Peale
- "The cyclone derives its powers from a calm center. So does a person."

Vince Lombardi
- "I've never known a man worth his salt who in the long run, deep down in his heart, didn't appreciate the grind, the discipline. There is something good in men that really yearns for discipline."

Zig Ziglar
- "Discipline yourself to do the things that you need to do when you need to do them, and the day will come when you will be able to do the things you want to do when you want to do them!"

19

Improve Your Attention, Awareness, Focus And Concentration To Excel At What You Do

Jerry's Tips:

- You cannot be a master of everything. Figure out what your talents, skills and desires can fuel you to being an expert in one area and then focus all of your attention and concentration every day to become the best you can be.

- Focus on details, but don't get stuck looking in the weeds; keep the big picture in sight.

- Don't do one thing and think about something else at the same time. Give 100% attention to whatever action you are performing. If you want to think about something else stop what you are doing and think about it.

- Focus all of your energy to succeed with your Plan A. Having a Plan B is for people who don't believe 100% in their Plan A.

Alexander Graham Bell
- "Concentrate all your thoughts on the task at hand. The sun's rays do not burn until brought to a focus."

Arnold Palmer
- "What do I mean by concentration? I mean focusing totally on the business at hand and commanding your body to do exactly what you want it to do."

Bruce Lee
- "The successful warrior is the average man, with laser-like focus."

IMPROVE YOUR ATTENTION, AWARENESS, FOCUS AND CONCENTRATION TO EXCEL AT WHAT YOU DO

- "Empty your mind, be formless. Shapeless, like water. If you put water into a cup, it becomes the cup. You put water into a bottle and it becomes the bottle. You put it in a teapot it becomes the teapot. Now, water can flow or it can crash. Be water my friend."

Jose Ortega y Gasset
- "Tell me to what you pay attention, and I will tell you who you are."

Miyamoto Musashi
- "Perception is strong and sight weak. In strategy it is important to see distant things as if they were close and to take a distanced view of close things."

Nido Qubein
- "Nothing can add more power to your life than concentrating all your energies on a limited set of targets."

Og Mandino
- "It is those who concentrate on but one thing at a time who advance in this world. The great man or woman is the one who never steps outside his or her specialty or foolishly dissipates his or her individuality."

Oprah Winfrey
- "Energy is the essence of life. Every day you decide how you're going to use it by knowing what you want and what it takes to reach that goal, and by maintaining focus."

P. T. Barnum
- "Engage in one type of business only, and stick to it faithfully until you succeed, or until your experience shows that you should abandon it."

- "A constant hammering on one nail will generally drive it home at last."

- "When a man's undivided attention is centered on one object, his mind will constantly be suggesting improvements of value, which would escape him if his brain was occupied by a dozen different subjects at once."

THE SUCCESS FORMULA FOR PERSONAL GROWTH

Pat Croce
- "Refrain from allowing your mind to wander toward other people's goals or to focus away from your own."

- "Stay Focused: Whenever I set out on a goal or mission, I pull out my mental magnifying glass, I hold it firmly and steadily above my goal, and I stay focused. All of my resources and energy are concentrated through the lens like a laser beam in the same direction, at the same intensity, and for the same purpose. Puff! It's amazing that when you focus on something with a burning desire — whether it's your job, your goal, your hobby, your health, the happiness of your loved ones — when you focus on it, you magnify it, making your goal more likely to become reality."

Robert J. Ringer
- "Laser like focus is perhaps the most common trademark of the super successful... If you aspire to play in the big leagues, you must be prepared to play every point as though it were match point. In other words, you have to be consistently focused. Dabblers are rarely, if ever, successful. It's when you focus totally, intensely, and consistently on one project -- a project that has the potential to yield a worthwhile payoff -- that you have the greatest chance of success."

Steve Jobs
- "People think focus means saying yes to the thing you've got to focus on. But that's not what it means at all. It means saying no to the hundred other good ideas that there are. You have to pick carefully."

Tony Robbins
- "One reason so few of us achieve what we truly want is that we never direct our focus; we never concentrate our power. Most people dabble their way through life, never deciding to master anything in particular."

- "Most people have no idea of the giant capacity we can immediately command when we focus all of our resources on mastering a single area of our lives."

W. Timothy Gallwey
- "Focus is the quintessential component of superior performance in every activity, no matter what the level of skill or the age of the performer."

IMPROVE YOUR ATTENTION, AWARENESS, FOCUS AND CONCENTRATION TO EXCEL AT WHAT YOU DO

William James

"Everyone knows what attention is. It is the taking possession by the mind, in clear and vivid form, of one out of what seem several simultaneously possible objects or trains of thought. Focalization, concentration of consciousness are of its essence. It implies withdrawal from some things in order to deal effectively with others, and is a condition which has a real opposite in the confused, dazed, scatterbrained state which in French is called distraction."

20

Preparation Is The Iceberg People Do Not See When They Notice You Are Successful

Jerry's Tips:

- You must prepare today and plan ahead to succeed tomorrow – there is no other method.

- Sharpening your saw is one hundred times more important than rushing off to cut down a tree with a dull saw.

- We do the way we practice. That means if you want to be successful at something, you must practice it with all the intensity and desire as if you were doing it for real because your 'real' performance is a 'reflection' of your 'practiced' actions.

- Remember, learning is indifferent to direction. If you practice something incorrectly or sloppily you will develop the habit of doing it incorrectly and that's how you will do it when you want to do it for real. That's why you must give 100% effort to your practice.

- If you learn from all of your preparation you will be ready for any challenge.

Abraham Lincoln
- "If I had six hours to chop down a tree, I'd spend the first hour sharpening the ax."

Alexander Graham Bell
- "Before anything else, preparation is the key to success."

Anonymous
- "Confidence and courage come through preparation and practice."

Preparation is the Iceberg People Do Not See When They Notice You Are Successful

- "It pays to plan ahead. It wasn't raining when Noah built the ark."

Arthur Ashe
- "One important key to success is self-confidence. An important key to self-confidence is preparation."

Benjamin Disraeli
- "One secret of success in life is for a man to be ready for his opportunity when it comes."

Benjamin Franklin
- "By failing to prepare, you are preparing to fail."

Bobby Fischer
- "I prepare myself well. I know what I can do before I go in. I'm always confident."

Bobby Knight
- "The will to succeed is important, but what's more important is the will to prepare."

Bruce Lee
- "I fear not the man who has practiced 10,000 kicks once, but I fear the man who has practiced one kick 10,000 times."

Confucius
- "Success depends upon previous preparation, and without such preparation there is sure to be failure."

Elbert Hubbard
- "The best preparation for good work tomorrow is to do good work today."

General Colin Powell
- "There are no secrets to success. It is the result of preparation, hard work, and learning from failure."

Joe Namath
- "What I do is prepare myself until I know I can do what I have to do."

THE SUCCESS FORMULA FOR PERSONAL GROWTH

Joe Paterno
- "The will to win is important, but the will to prepare is vital."

John Dewey
- "Arriving at one goal is the starting point to another."

John Wooden
- "Failing to prepare is preparing to fail."

Mark Spitz
- "If you fail to prepare, you're prepared to fail."

Mark Zupan
- "An opportunity is worth to a person exactly what their preparation enables them to make it."

Michael Caine
- "Rehearsal is the work, performance is the relaxation."

Muhammad Ali
- "I hated every minute of training, but I said, 'Don't quit. Suffer now and live the rest of your life as a champion.'"

Pete Rose
- "My father taught me that the only way you can make good at anything is to practice, and then practice some more. It's easy to practice something you're good at, and that's what most people do. What's tough is to go out and work hard on things you don't do very well."

Robert J. Ringer
- "If you're prepared, then you're able to feel confident."

Roger Maris
- "You win not by chance, but by preparation."

- "You hit home runs not by chance but by preparation."

Roger Staubach
- "Spectacular achievements are always preceded by unspectacular preparation."

PREPARATION IS THE ICEBERG PEOPLE DO NOT SEE WHEN THEY NOTICE YOU ARE SUCCESSFUL

Serena and Venus Williams
- "To become really great at something, you have to repeat it over and over so you can really ace it."

William Osler
- "The best preparation for tomorrow is to do today's work superbly well."

Vince Lombardi
- "Practice does not make perfect. Only perfect practice makes perfect."

Zig Ziglar
- "Anything worth doing, is worth doing poorly until you do it well."

21

Conduct An Honest Self-Assessment

Jerry's Tips:

- The first step to improving anything, especially yourself, is to know where you are currently at.

- Recognize the great gifts and uniqueness that you have and don't worry about what you currently don't have.

- What are your personal strengths and talents?

- What interests you? What do you like to do? What would you like to be very good at?

- What do you have now? What do you need to achieve your goals?

- Figure out how to maximize your strengths and talents; they are your competitive advantage.

- Be honest about what's not working well, or needs improvement in your life, and how to improve it.

- Know and work on your weaknesses; but realize you can't do everything perfectly.

Anonymous

- "If you haven't all the things you want, be grateful for the things you don't have that you wouldn't want."

- "I once cried when I had no shoes until I saw a man who had no feet."

Conduct an Honest Self-Assessment

Bruce Lee
- "Mistakes are always forgivable, if one has the courage to admit them."

Charles Dickens
- "Reflect upon your present blessings of which every man has many - not on your past misfortunes, of which all men have some."

Dale Carnegie
- "If only the people who worry about their liabilities would think about the riches they do possess, they would stop worrying."

Donald Trump
- "What is your creative capital?"

- "What do you have to offer?"

- "What have you acquired in your experience and in your studies that makes you valuable?"

- "Are you aware of your own potential?"

- "Will you be equipped to make a difference when the time comes for you to step forward?"

Henry Van Dyke
- "Use what talents you possess; the woods would be very silent if no birds sang except those that sang best."

Jack Welch
- "Face reality as it is, not as it was or as you wish it to be."

Les Brown
- "Just because Fate doesn't deal you the right cards, it doesn't mean you should give up. It just means you have to play the cards you get to their maximum potential."

John Wooden
- "Don't let what you can't do stop you from doing what you can do."

Malcolm S. Forbes
- "Too many people overvalue what they are not and undervalue what they are."

Norman Vincent Peale
- "One of the greatest moments in anybody's developing experience is when he no longer tries to hide from himself but determines to get acquainted with himself as he really is."

Pat Croce
- "If you look long enough and hard enough, you'll find something you're good at."

Robert J. Ringer
- "Reality isn't the way you wish things to be, nor the way they appear to be, but the way they actually are."

Theodore Roosevelt
- "Do what you can, with what you have, where you are."

Tony Robbins
- "Awareness is the foremost power."

Vince Lombardi
- "The measure of who we are is what we do with what we have."

Winston Churchill
- "The truth is incontrovertible, malice may attack it, ignorance may deride it, but in the end; there it is."

Zig Ziglar
- "It's not what you've got, it's what you use that makes a difference."

22

Develop Your Vision Statement, Live Your Life On Purpose Not By Accident

Jerry's Tips:

- Close your eyes and imagine how you would like your life to be when it comes to an end. What would make you content and fulfilled to have accomplished and provided for your loved ones? Now open your eyes and look around. If what you are doing now is not going to get you there, change what you are doing to achieve that vision.

- Vision is what you desire as the big picture of your life; it's your life's purpose.

- Create your vision and determine your life's purpose.

- The meaning of life is to fulfill your purpose.

- Without a clear purpose you will end up following someone else's purpose for you. And they probably don't have anything good in mind for you.

- Don't live your life by throwing dice. Know your purpose, what you want to accomplish in life and start working to get it.

- Align your thoughts, feelings and actions with your values to achieve your goals and create your vision.

THE SUCCESS FORMULA FOR PERSONAL GROWTH

Alfred A. Montapert
"In life, the first thing you must do is decide what you really want. Weigh the costs and the results. Are the results worthy of the costs? Then make up your mind completely and go after your goal with all your might."

Bob Proctor
"All of the great achievers of the past have been visionary figures; they were men and women who projected into the future. They thought of what could be, rather than what already was, and then they moved themselves into action, to bring these things into fruition."

Brian Tracy
"A clear vision, backed by definite plans, gives you a tremendous feeling of confidence and personal power."

Donald Trump
"We all have a purpose in life, and that's to do our best to live up to our potential. It's really pretty simple. All we have to do is tune in to our talents and capabilities. Remember, I didn't say it was easy-- I said it was simple."

Douglas Lurtan
"When you determine what you want, you have made the most important decision in your life. You have to know what you want in order to attain it."

Jack Canfield
"One of the main reasons why most people don't get what they want is they haven't decided what they want."

James Allen
"To put away aimlessness and weakness, and to begin to think with purpose, is to enter the ranks of those strong ones who only recognize failure as one of the pathways to attainment; who make all conditions serve them, and who think strongly, attempt fearlessly, and accomplish masterfully."

John C. Maxwell
"Someone once said there are two great days in life – the day you were born and the day you discover why."

DEVELOP YOUR VISION STATEMENT
LIVE YOUR LIFE ON PURPOSE NOT BY ACCIDENT

Pat Croce

- "What do you want? What do you want to do? What do you want to become? What is your vision for the future? What idea, invention, or endeavor do you want to create?
  If you can't answer these questions immediately – or if your response is the all too familiar 'I don't know' or 'I wish I knew' – then you're on the short road to nowhere. And you're not alone."

- "What do you want to accomplish in life? What are you good at? Your purpose is the intersection of desire, talent, passion and ability."

- "If you live for nothing in particular, then you'll settle for anything in general."

- "If you don't know what you want to do with your life, you cannot make a realistic plan to get it."

Tony Robbins

- "Create a vision and never let the environment, other people's beliefs, or the limits of what has been done in the past shape your decisions. Ignore conventional wisdom."

- "Achievement results in meaningful success only if it's consistent with your values and in-service to your goals."

- "Your vision must inspire you to take action to achieve it."

23

Set Major Goals That Give Your Life Purpose, Direction And Meaning

Jerry's Tips:

- A goal is an objective you want to achieve and by when. Another word for an objective is a result.

- Your current situation in life is the result of your current goals or lack of goals. If you want to change your circumstances, change your goals.

- Football, soccer, hockey and water polo have goal posts so the teams know where to aim to win. You too need goals, without them you don't know where to focus your energies to achieve what you want.

- We are all on a personal journey and we need to know where we want to go or else we will never get there.

- If you live your life without goals and plans to reach them, you will drift like a ship without a rudder and never reach a happy destination.

- The successful person can answer the questions: what are your ambitions, aspirations, goals, plans, and vision?

- Successful people have major goals that get them what they want out of life and they think every day how to achieve them.

- Desire to improve your life and then creating a plan to accomplish your goals are the most powerful ingredients to make yourself successful.

- A goal without a deadline is nothing more than a dream or wish.

SET MAJOR GOALS THAT GIVE YOUR LIFE PURPOSE, DIRECTION AND MEANING

- Learn to set goals with self-imposed deadlines and targets and reward yourself whenever you achieve one.

- Progress is made one step at a time. Don't think about how large a goal is; keep taking one small step after another and you will get there.

- Do not be discouraged by the difficulty to accomplish a large goal; break it into smaller goals and tasks and create a timeline for finishing them.

- The only way to eat an elephant is one bite at a time. Break your goals into smaller goals and steps, and then into bite size tasks.

- Objectives a/k/a tasks are planned steps to reach your goals.

- When you align your dreams, to your goals, actions and desire, success is the result.

- Goals provide meaning to your life. People are meant to pursue challenges, not to just exist and eat cake.

- To be happy and not bored make sure you always have a personally important goal you are working towards.

- An important goal gives you a reason to jump out of bed when you wake up each day!

- Focusing on your goals prevents you from wasting time on unproductive and unhealthy distractions.

- What you get by achieving your goals is not as important as the type of person you become by achieving your goals.

- In order to improve, you must set goals that you need to stretch a bit to reach.

Anonymous
- "The whole world steps aside for the man who knows where he is going."

Aristotle
- "Man is a goal seeking animal. His life only has meaning if he is reaching out and striving for his goals."

Arnold H. Glasow
- "In life, as in football, you won't go far unless you know where the goal posts are."

Ben Stein
- "The indispensable first step to getting the things you want out of life is this: decide what you want."

Benjamin Ewise
- "It must be borne in the mind that the tragedy of life does not lie in not reaching your goal; the tragedy is in not having a goal to reach. Not a calamity to die without dreams not fulfilled but a calamity not to dream. Not a disaster to be unable to capture your ideal; it is a disaster not to have an ideal to capture. Not a disgrace not to reach the stars but a disgrace to have no stars to reach. Not failure but low aim is sin."

Bo Jackson
- "Set your goals high and don't stop 'til you get there."

Bob Proctor
- "If you know what to do to reach your goal, it's not a big enough goal."

- "Your purpose explains what you are doing with your life. Your vision explains how you are living your purpose. Your goals enable you to realize your vision."

Bruce Lee
- "A goal is not always meant to be reached, it often serves simply as something to aim at."

Charles (Tremendous) Jones
- "Everyone has a success mechanism and a failure mechanism. The failure mechanism goes off by itself. The success mechanism only goes off with a goal. Every time we write down and talk about a goal, we push the button to start the success mechanism."

SET MAJOR GOALS THAT GIVE YOUR LIFE PURPOSE, DIRECTION AND MEANING

Catherine Pulsifer
- "Goals help focus you on areas in both your personal and professional life that are important and meaningful, rather than being guided by what other people want you to be, do, or accomplish."

- "The unfortunate aspect about living life without your own goals is that you may very well reach a point in your life where you will wonder, 'what would have happened if I had only done...'"

Charles C. Noble
- "You must have long term goals to keep you from being frustrated by short term failures."

David J. Schwartz
- "A goal is an objective, a purpose. A goal is more than a dream; it's a dream being acted upon. A goal is more than a hazy 'oh, I wish I could.' A goal is a clear 'This is what I'm working toward.'"

- "Without goals individuals just wander through life. They stumble along, never knowing where they are going, so they never get anywhere."

- "Goals are as essential to success as air is to life. No one ever stumbles into success without a goal. No one ever lives without air. Get a clear fix on where you want to go."

Denis Waitley
- "The secret to productive goal setting is in establishing clearly defined goals, writing them down and then focusing on them several times a day with words, pictures and emotions as if we've already achieved them."

- "The reason most people never reach their goals is that they don't define them, or ever seriously consider them as believable or achievable. Winners can tell you where they are going, what they plan to do along the way, and who will be sharing the adventure with them."

Earl Nightingale
- "To achieve happiness, we should make certain that we are never without an important goal."

THE SUCCESS FORMULA FOR PERSONAL GROWTH

- "People with goals succeed, because they know where they're going. It's that simple."

- "Your problem is to bridge the gap which exists between where you are now and the goal you intend to reach."

Elbert Hubbard
- "Many people fail in life, not for lack of ability or brains or even courage but simply because they have never organized their energies around a goal."

Greg Anderson
- "When we are motivated by goals that have deep meaning, by dreams that need completion, by pure love that needs expressing, then we truly live."

Henry Ford
- "Nothing is particularly hard if you divide it into small jobs."

Henry David Thoreau
- "In the long run men hit only what they aim at."

J. C. Penney
- "Give me a stock clerk with a goal and I'll give you a man who will make history. Give me a man with no goals and I'll give you a stock clerk."

Jim Rohn
- "The major reason for setting a goal is for what it makes of you to accomplish it. What it makes of you will always be the far greater value than what you get."

- "The ultimate reason for setting goals is to entice you to become the person it takes to achieve them."

- "We all need lots of powerful long-range goals to help us past the short-term obstacles."

- "If you go to work on your goals your goals will go to work on you. If you go to work on your plan, your plan will go to work on you. Whatever good things we build end up building us."

- "Set goals and achieve them for what it makes of you to attain them."

SET MAJOR GOALS THAT GIVE YOUR LIFE PURPOSE, DIRECTION AND MEANING

- "Never underestimate just how important it is to have very specific, concrete goals. They act as magnets that draw you toward them!"

Julius Irving
- "Goals determine what you're going to be."

Kiana Tom
- "I am a goal setter and I set more goals everyday. I keep lists of goals in my office to stay on track."

Kurt Lewin
- "A successful individual typically sets his next goal somewhat but not too much above his last achievement. In this way he steadily raises his level of aspiration."

Kurt Thomas
- "I feel that the most important step in any major accomplishment is setting a specific goal. This enables you to keep your mind focused on your goal and off the many obstacles that will arise when you're striving to do your best."

Les Brown
- "Goals help you channel your energy into action."

- "Life takes on meaning when you become motivated, set goals and charge after them in an unstoppable manner."

- "Review your goals twice every day in order to be focused on achieving them."

- "Most people fail in life not because they aimed too high and missed. Most people fail in life because they aimed too low and hit. And many don't aim at all."

Mark Victor Hansen
- "You control your future, your destiny. What you think about comes about. By recording your dreams and goals on paper, you set in motion the process of becoming the person you most want to be. Put your future in good hands – your own."

THE SUCCESS FORMULA FOR PERSONAL GROWTH

Dr. Maxwell Maltz
- "Emptiness is a symptom that you are not living creatively. You either have not a goal that is important enough to you, or you are not using your talents and efforts in a striving toward an important goal."

- "People who say that life is not worthwhile are really saying that they themselves have no personal goals which are worthwhile. Get yourself a goal worth working for. Better still, get yourself a project. Always have something ahead of you to 'look forward to' – to work for and to hope for."

- "We are built to conquer environment, solve problems, achieve goals, and we find no real satisfaction or happiness in life without obstacles to conquer and goals to achieve."

Michelangelo
- "The greater danger for most of us lies not in setting our aim too high and falling short; but in setting our aim too low, and achieving our mark."

Muhammad Ali
- "What keeps me going is goals."

Napoleon Hill
- "A goal is a dream with a deadline."

- "The world has the habit of making room for the man whose words and actions show that he knows where he is going."

Nido Qubein
- "Winners compare their achievements with their goals, while losers compare their achievements with those of other people."

- "When a goal matters enough to a person, that person will find a way to accomplish what at first seemed impossible."

Og Mandino
- "The victory of success is half won when one gains the habit of setting goals and achieving them. Even the most tedious chore will become endurable as you parade through each day convinced that every task, no matter how menial or boring, brings you closer to fulfilling your dreams."

SET MAJOR GOALS THAT GIVE YOUR LIFE PURPOSE, DIRECTION AND MEANING

- "Set goals for the day, the week, the month, the year, and your life."

Oprah Winfrey
- "The big secret in life is that there is no big secret. Whatever your goal, you can get there if you're willing to work."

- "If you want to accomplish the goals of your life, you have to begin with the spirit."

Pat Croce
- "When you identify a goal you want to achieve carefully consider whether you genuinely want to achieve it, or is it something that someone else wants you to achieve?"

Ralph Waldo Emerson
- "We aim above the mark to hit the mark."

- "The world makes way for the man who knows where he is going."

Steve Garvey
- "You have to set goals that are almost out of reach. If you set a goal that is attainable without much work or thought, you are stuck with something below your true talent and potential."

Susan Polis Schutz
- "If you have a goal in life that takes a lot of energy, that requires a lot of work, that incurs a great deal of interest and that is a challenge to you, you will always look forward to waking up to see what the new day brings."

Ted Williams
- "A man has to have goals - for a day, for a lifetime - and that was mine, to have people say, 'There goes Ted Williams, the greatest hitter who ever lived.'"

Thomas Carlyle
- "A man without a goal is a ship without a rudder. You don't know where you are going."

Tom Landry
- "Setting a goal is not the main thing. It is deciding how you will go about achieving it and staying with that plan."

THE SUCCESS FORMULA FOR PERSONAL GROWTH

Tony Robbins

- "Setting goals is the first step in turning the invisible into the visible."

- "People are not lazy. They simply have impotent goals - that is, goals that do not inspire them."

- "Goals are a means to an end, not the ultimate purpose of our lives. They are simply a tool to concentrate our focus and move us in a direction. The only reason we really pursue goals is to cause ourselves to expand and grow. Achieving goals by themselves will never make us happy in the long term; it's who you become, as you overcome the obstacles necessary to achieve your goals, that can give you the deepest and most long-lasting sense of fulfillment."

- "Getting a goal is not enough. You need to associate strong emotions with it that flow through your body. You need to have emotions associated with what you want. A goal with emotion will 'pull' you to put the effort in to achieve your goals."

- "The most important thing you can do to achieve your goals is to make sure that as soon as you set them, you immediately begin to create momentum. The most important rules that I ever adopted to help me in achieving my goals were those I learned from a very successful man who taught me to first write down the goal, and then to never leave the site of setting a goal without first taking some form of positive action toward its attainment."

W. Clement Stone

- "No matter how carefully you plan your goals they will never be more than pipe dreams unless you pursue them with gusto."

- "To solve a problem or to reach a goal, you don't need to know all the answers in advance. But you must have a clear idea of the problem or the goal you want to reach."

Zig Ziglar

- "You must have a goal because it's just as difficult to reach a destination you don't have, as it is to come back from a place you've never been."

- "What you get by achieving your goals is not as important as what you become by achieving your goals."

SET MAJOR GOALS THAT GIVE YOUR LIFE PURPOSE, DIRECTION AND MEANING

- "A goal properly set is halfway reached."

- "Goals are dreams we convert to plans and take action to fulfill."

- "The basic goal-reaching principle is to understand that you go as far as you can see, and when you get there you will always be able to see farther."

24

Create A Written Plan To Achieve Your Goals And Reach Your Vision

Jerry's Tips:

- A plan is your specific steps to accomplish your goal.

- A goal that is not written down is just an idea that might fade away. Writing it down makes it permanent.

- Write your goals down to breath life into them.

- Having written goals is not enough. You must write your goals down in detail and assign deadlines to complete them.

- The plans and goals of most people and businesses fail and are not accomplished unless they have specific written realty based execution steps to get you from where you are to where you want to go.

- Written plans improve the likelihood of a successful outcome.

  An architect would not start to build a building without written blueprints; a ship's captain would not start an ocean voyage without a map, an airline's pilot would not start a flight without a written flight plan and a movie producer would not start filming a film without a written script.

  In the same way, you must have a written plan that shows the steps of how you will achieve your goals.

- A written plan increases your motivation to work on your goal because it reminds you of your goal.

- A written plan lets you see how you are going to get from where you are to completing your goal. It will let you see if you missed a step.

CREATE A WRITTEN PLAN TO ACHIEVE YOUR GOALS AND REACH YOUR VISION

- A written plan gives us a way to mark and measure your progress toward completing a goal.

- Each time you mark a step completed in your plan to achieve a goal you will feel more confident and energized to accomplish your goal.

Lee Iacocca
- "The discipline of writing something down is the first step toward making it happen."

Napoleon Hill
- "Reduce your plan to writing. The moment you complete this, you will have definitely given concrete form to the intangible desire."

25

Commitment

Make An Unshakeable Promise To Yourself To Achieve Your Goals

Jerry's Tips:

- Commitment is not just saying 'yes' to something; it's mentally buying shares of stock in whatever you do and pledging yourself to do whatever is required to make them worth something by accomplishing your goal.

- Until you commit to something you think you can back out. After you commit there's no turning back!

- Commitment comes after your decision to do something and before you take action to achieve it.

- Once you are committed to something you will find a way to make it happen.

- Renew your commitment to your goals each day by reminding yourself of the benefits you will have when you achieve them.

COMMITMENT
MAKE AN UNSHAKEABLE PROMISE TO YOURSELF TO ACHIEVE YOUR GOALS

Anonymous
- "Commitment separates the doers from the dreamers."

Art Turock
- "There's a difference between interest and commitment. When you're interested in doing something, you do it only when circumstances permit. When you're committed to something, you accept no excuses, only results."

Og Mandino
- "When high achievers use the term 'hard work' they mean working at top capacity for seventy or eighty hours, or more, every week, loving their work until it becomes a driving passion, and devoting all their waking hours to thinking, planning, and striving toward goals which others consider impossible. Total commitment!"

Pat Riley
- "There are only two options regarding commitment. You're either in or out. There's no such thing as a life in-between."

Peter Drucker
- "Unless commitment is made, there are only promises and hopes... but no plans."

Terry Bradshaw
- "The life of a winner is the result of an unswervering commitment to a never ending process of self completion."

Tony Robbins
- "I believe life is constantly testing us for our level of commitment, and life's greatest rewards are reserved for those who demonstrate a never-ending commitment to act until they achieve. This level of resolve can move mountains, but it must be constant and consistent. As simplistic as this may sound, it is still the common denominator separating those who live their dreams from those who live in regret."

- "There is always a way - if you're committed."

- "There's no abiding success without commitment."

- "If you develop the absolute sense of certainty that powerful beliefs provide, then you can get yourself to accomplish virtually anything, including those things that other people are certain are impossible."

Vince Lombardi
- "The quality of a person's life is in direct proportion to their commitment to excellence, regardless of their chosen field of endeavor."

- "Once a man has made a commitment to a way of life, he puts the greatest strength in the world behind him. It's something we call heart power. Once a man has made this commitment, nothing will stop him short of success."

- "Unless a man believes in himself and makes a total commitment to his career and puts everything he has into it - his mind, his body, his heart - what's life worth to him?"

W.H. Murray
- "Until you are committed, there is hesitancy, the chance to draw back, ineffectiveness. It is true: the moment one definitely commits oneself, then Providence moves. All sorts of things begin to happen to help you that would never otherwise have occurred. A whole stream of events issues from that decision, raising in your favor all manner of unforeseen incidents, meetings and material assistance, which you couldn't have dreamt would come your way."

26

Expect Success

Jerry's Tips:

- Expectations prime-the-pump to produce desired results.

- Carry a deep feeling that your great success is inevitable because you are committed to work as hard as you can to achieve your goals.

- High expectations lead to high achievement.

Andrew Carnegie
- "Think of yourself as on the threshold of unparalleled success. A whole clear, glorious life lies before you. Achieve! Achieve!"

Anonymous
- "We tend to find what we look for: good or evil, problems or solutions."

Brian Tracy
- "Whatever we expect with confidence becomes our own self-fulfilling prophecy."

- "We will always tend to fulfill our own expectation of ourselves."

Denis Waitley
- "Expect the best; convert problems into opportunities."

Earl Nightingale
- "We tend to live up to our expectations."

Giovanni Niccolini
- "By asking for the impossible we obtain the best possible."

J. P. Morgan
- "When you expect things to happen - strangely enough - they do happen."

Joe Montana
- "Winners, I am convinced, imagine their dreams first. They want it with all their heart and expect it to come true. There is, I believe, no other way to live."

Joe Paterno
- "Act like you expect to get into the end zone."

Michael Jordan
- "You have to expect things of yourself before you can do them."

Norman Vincent Peale
- "We tend to get what we expect."

Orison Swett Marden
- "Every child should be taught to expect success."

Pat Croce
- "Expect the best, expect success. Our efforts tend to match our expectations. You control your thoughts and you control your world. It's your choice. Positive, passionate, persistent thoughts can take you to the top."

- "I know that when you enthusiastically pursue your heart's desire with a focused determination and an expectation of success, the world will create circumstances and opportunities for the fulfillment of your dreams and goals.

  Notice that I didn't say wish, want, hope, or pray for success…although prayer helps. I'm telling you to pursue your heart's desires with a mindset of expecting success. And let this philosophy/attitude saturate every cell in your body – in your facial expressions, body language, speech patterns, posture, personality, and your approach to life."

EXPECT SUCCESS

- "People want to win, but most of them expect to lose. They want to be rich, but they expect to be in debt. They want to be thin, but they expect to be overweight. They want to be leaders, but they expect to be followers. They want to feel great, but they expect to feel okay or getting by. I'm telling you that you must mentally expect success. Because whether you think you can or you think you can't – you're right!"

Sam Walton
- "High expectations are the key to everything."

Samuel Smiles
- "An intense anticipation itself transforms possibility into reality; our desires being often but precursors of the things which we are capable of performing."

27

Remain Flexible And Adapt As You Execute Your Plan

Jerry's Tips:

- Successful people know that it's not enough to simply follow their beautiful looking written plan to achieve their goal.

- Successful people know you need to work your plan, which means to continually adjust it as needed based on events to reach your goal.

- Never think you have failed simply because your progress does not match the perfect picture in your plan.

- A plan is not guaranteed to be perfect. It's like life – live, learn and adjust on a daily basis.

- Don't fall into the trap of thinking that a plan is guaranteed to be perfect. Plans are like life – live it, work it, continually learn and adjust on a daily basis. The key is to keep your eye on your goals and expect to make constant adjustments to make progress in their general direction.

- A plan set in cement is guaranteed to sink and not produce success.

- A plan should not be viewed as a guarantee of what will occur when you execute it.

- A plan always shows your path to achieve a goal as a straight line. But that's not how life works.

REMAIN FLEXIBLE AND ADAPT AS YOU EXECUTE YOUR PLAN

- Like a ship at sea, plans and achievements do not always go in a straight direction. They zig zag and encounter setbacks and obstacles – just keep adjusting to keep them headed in the intended direction. Make sure that despite any detours in your life or your plans, that you focus on heading in the direction of your goals, and you are guaranteed to reach them!

- In life, you will always encounter problems and obstacles that will cause your progress to zig zag and sometimes go backwards before moving forward again.

- The skill of a successful person is not in the impossible ability to eliminate all problems before they arise, but to meet and work out difficulties when they do arise.

- Problems and delays are part of life. Be ready to respond to them and you will achieve your goal.

- Strategic planning, adopting specific steps to achieve your short and long term goals is very important; but then, executing constant, focused daily action in service to your goals will determine if you succeed or fail to achieve them.

- Creating your strategic plan is extremely important, but making the plan work is an even bigger challenge than creating the plan.

- All plan and little or no action is a recipe for failure. You must learn to plan and execute your plan to achieve your goals.

- Planning never ends; at first you plan to create your plan and then you must continue to plan as you execute your plan and adjust to circumstances.

Anonymous
- "If you fail to plan, you plan to fail."

Bruce Lee
- "Notice that the stiffest tree is most easily cracked, while the bamboo or willow survives by bending with the wind."

- "All fixed set patterns are incapable of adaptability or pliability. The truth is outside of all fixed patterns."

Catherine Pulsifer
- "Do not be discouraged if your plans do not succeed the first time. No one learns to walk by taking only one step."

Confucius
- "When it is obvious that the goals cannot be reached, don't adjust the goals, adjust the action steps."

David J. Schwartz
- "Persistence in one way is not a guarantee of victory. But persistence blended with experimentation does guarantee success."

- "Many ambitious people go through life with admirable persistence and show of ambition, but they fail to succeed because they don't experiment with new approaches. Stay with your goal. Don't waver an inch from it. But don't beat you head against wall. If you aren't getting results, try a new approach."

- "Edison created the electric light bulb. It's reported that he conducted thousands of experiments before he invented the electric light bulb. But note, Edison conducted experiments. He persisted in his goal to develop a light bulb. But he made that persistence pay off by blending it with experimentation."

- "Oil companies persistently drill hundreds of oil wells to look for oil. But when they are sure a well is a dry hole they alter their approach and drill a new will – their persistence is not bull headed."

Donald Trump
- "It is equally important to plan and to remain flexible."

Napoleon Hill
- "The majority of men meet with failure because of their lack of persistence in creating new plans to take the place of those which fail."

- "When defeat comes, accept it as a signal that your plans are not sound, rebuild those plans, and set sail once more toward your coveted goal."

REMAIN FLEXIBLE AND ADAPT AS YOU EXECUTE YOUR PLAN

Robert Burns
- "The best laid plans of mice and men often go astray."

Pat Croce
- "Paint your vision, develop tasks, prioritize action steps and do it now."

- "The more precise you plan, the less surprise will be your success."

Publilius Syrus
- "It is a bad plan that admits of no modification."

Will Rogers
- "Plans get you into things but you must work your way out."

Zig Ziglar
- "Expect the best. Prepare for the worst. Capitalize on what comes."

28

Don't Procrastinate To Start On Your Goals And Focus Time Every Day To Work On Them

Jerry's Tips:

- If you don't start you can't succeed.

- Don't focus so much on planning your success that you never get around to executing on your plan.

- Once you have decided what you want to do, you must then start to do it and not keep thinking about it.

- There will never be the perfect time to take action to succeed.

- Don't wait for inspiration to take action to achieve your goals.

- You may know in every molecule of your mind and body what to do to succeed, but until you actually get out there and do the work you're just dreaming.

- Thought is not enough to succeed – planning is not enough. Only taking action will produce results that achieve your goal.

- Your vision, ideas, goals and plans are useless unless you take action to implement them.

- Don't put off taking action to achieve your goals because you are trying to create a perfect plan. Start today and keep getting better.

- Right now is always the best time to start anything.

- Do today what you are thinking about doing tomorrow.

DON'T PROCRASTINATE TO START TO WORK ON YOUR GOALS AND FOCUS TIME EVERY DAY TO WORK ON THEM

- Don't wait for tomorrow to do something, because when tomorrow arrives it will be today again and you'll want to put it off.

- When you catch yourself being lazy immediately snap yourself out of it by thinking positive thoughts. Remind yourself of the benefits you'll get by not being lazy, and take action to accomplish something.

- To start to break your procrastination habit pick something you have been putting off and start doing a very small amount of it so you know it will be easy to do. Accomplishing that small amount will motivate you to continue and do more… and more.

- Don't put doing something off because you think you will not do it well. Successful people know the key is that it's more important that you 'start' and then you will improve.

Anonymous
- "No rules for success will work if you don't."

- "Ideas are a dime a dozen. People who put them into action are priceless."

Benjamin Franklin
- "Don't put off until tomorrow what you can do today."

Bruce Lee
- "If you spend too much time thinking about a thing, you'll never get it done."

- "If you want to learn to swim jump into the water. On dry land no frame of mind is ever going to help you."

Catherine Pulsifer
- "Rather than thinking 'if and when', start doing, take action, stop talking about 'if and when'."

David J. Schwartz
- "We must be willing to make an intelligent compromise with perfection lest we wait forever before taking action."

THE SUCCESS FORMULA FOR PERSONAL GROWTH

- "Tell yourself, I'm in condition right now to begin. I can't gain a thing by putting it off. I'll use the 'get ready' time and energy to 'get going' instead."

- "Remember: thinking in terms of 'now' gets things accomplished. But thinking in terms of 'someday' or 'sometime' usually means failure."

- "Success shuns the man who lacks ideas. But let's make no mistakes about this point either. Ideas in themselves are not enough. Ideas alone won't bring success. Ideas are only of value when they are acted on."

- "There are two types of people in the world. Successful people take action, get things done, follow through on ideas and plans. Average and mediocre people are passive: they postpone doing things until proved he shouldn't or can't do them until it's too late."

Donald Trump
- "There is a greater chance of success if you actually try to do something versus doing nothing."

Frank Tibolt
- "We should be taught not to wait for inspiration to start a thing. Action always generates inspiration. Inspiration seldom generates action."

General Colin Powell
- "A dream doesn't become reality through magic; it takes sweat, determination and hard work."

General George S. Patton
- "A good plan today is better than a perfect plan tomorrow."

- "A good plan executed with vigor right now beats a 'perfect' plan executed next week."

Georges Bernanos
- "A thought which does not result in an action is nothing much, and an action which does not proceed from a thought is nothing at all."

Jackie Collins
- "If you want to be a writer - stop talking about it and sit down and write! That applies to anything in life."

DON'T PROCRASTINATE TO START TO WORK ON YOUR GOALS AND FOCUS TIME EVERY DAY TO WORK ON THEM

Japanese Proverb
- "Vision without action is a daydream. Action without vision is a nightmare."

Jim Rohn
- "The opposite of perseverance is procrastination. Perseverance means you never quit. Procrastination usually means you never get started, although the inability to finish something is also a form of procrastination."

Joe Dimaggio
- "If you keep thinking about what you want to do or what you hope will happen, you don't do it, and it won't happen."

John C. Maxwell
- "An idea is worthless unless you use it."

John Wanamaker
- "Nothing comes merely by thinking about it."

Lao Tzu
- "A journey of a thousand miles begins with a single step."

Lee Iacocca
- "Apply yourself. Get all the education you can, but then, by God, do something. Don't just stand there, make it happen."
- "So what do we do? Anything. Something. So long as we just don't sit there. If we screw it up, start over. Try something else. If we wait until we've satisfied all the uncertainties, it may be too late."

Leonardo da Vinci
- "I have been impressed with the urgency of doing. Knowing is not enough; we must apply. Being willing is not enough; we must do."

Les Brown
- "You don't have to be great to get started, but you have to get started to be great."
- "The time is 'now' to do something – don't drag your feet."

THE SUCCESS FORMULA FOR PERSONAL GROWTH

Mark Victor Hansen

- "Don't wait until everything is just right. It will never be perfect. There will always be challenges, obstacles and less than perfect conditions. So what. Get started now. With each step you take, you will grow stronger and stronger, more and more skilled, more and more self-confident and more and more successful."

- "You don't have to get it perfect, you just have to get it going."

Mark Twain

- "The secret of getting ahead is getting started. The secret of getting started is breaking your complex overwhelming tasks into small manageable tasks, and then starting on the first one."

Martin Luther King, Jr.

- "Take the first step in faith. You don't have to see the whole staircase, just take the first step."

Mary Kay Ash

- "Ideas are a dime a dozen, but the men and women who implement them are priceless."

Michael Jordan

- "Some people want it to happen, some wish it would happen, others make it happen."

Miyamoto Musashi

- "Do not waste time idling or thinking after you have set your goals."

Napoleon Bonaparte

- "Take time to deliberate; but when the time for action arrives, stop thinking and go in."

Napoleon Hill

- "Create a definite plan for carrying out your desire and begin at once, whether you ready or not, to put this plan into action."

- "Don't wait. The time will never be just right."

- "Procrastination is the bad habit of putting of until the day after tomorrow what should have been done the day before yesterday."

Don't Procrastinate to Start to Work on Your Goals and Focus Time Every Day to Work on Them

Nike Sneaker Company
- "Just Do IT!"

- "No matter what the task, if it feels onerous and is pushing all your procrastination buttons, but you know it has to get done, stop making excuses. JUST DO IT!"

Nolan Bushnell
- "Everyone who's ever taken a shower has an idea. It's the person who gets out of the shower, dries off and does something about it who makes a difference."

Og Mandino
- "I will live this day as if it is my last."

- "Tomorrow is only found in the calendar of fools."

- "Success and procrastination are absolutely incompatible. In order to succeed you must, and you can, cure yourself of putting things off."

- "I will act now. I will act now. I will act now. I will repeat these words again and again and again, each hour, each day, every day, until the words become as much a habit as my breathing and the actions which follow become as instinctive as the blinking of my eyelids. With these words I can condition my mind to perform every act necessary for my success."

Pablo Picasso
- "Only put off until tomorrow what you are willing to die having left undone."

- "Action is the foundational key to all success."

Robert Collier
- "Take the first step, and your mind will mobilize all its forces to your aid. But the first essential is that you begin. Once the battle is started, all that is within and without you will come to your assistance."

Tony Robbins
- "In life, lots of people know what to do, but few people actually do what they know. Knowing is not enough! You must take action."

THE SUCCESS FORMULA FOR PERSONAL GROWTH

- "Some people dream of success while others wake up and work hard at it."

- "It not knowing what to do, it's doing what you know."

- "The path to success is to take massive, determined action."

Wayne Dyer
- "Procrastination is one of the most common and deadliest of diseases and its toll on success and happiness is heavy."

- "Resolving to do something in the future which you could do now is an acceptable substitute for doing it, and permits you to delude yourself that you are really not compromising yourself by not doing what you have set out to do."

Will Rogers
- "Even if you're on the right track, you'll get run over if you just sit there."

W. Clement Stone
- "So many fail because they don't get started -- they don't go. They don't overcome inertia. They don't begin."

William Faulkner
- "The man who removes a mountain begins by carrying away small stones."

Zig Ziglar
- "Those who wait until all the lights are on green before starting will never leave home."

29

Track And Measure Your Progress Towards Achieving Your Goals

Jerry's Tips:

- For a successful life, or successful business, measure what you want to improve.

- Measure your progress towards achieving your goals.

- The lessons from business and sports apply to your life; you can't succeed unless you measure the right things and do something about what you learn from the measurement to bring you closer to achieving your goal.

- Once you know your goals you should measure your progress to achieve them. Seeing your favorable progress will serve as positive reinforcement to continue your hard work and seeing negative progress will alert you to something you should change to get you back on track.

- Measure the quality of your life. You can define quality any way you want but you should have a definition of what it means for 'you' to have a quality life.

- There is no one right way to measure your progress. Any way you decide to do it will work. The important point is that you do some type of measurement.

Albert Einstein

- "Not everything that can be counted counts, and not everything that counts can be counted."

THE SUCCESS FORMULA FOR PERSONAL GROWTH

Dr. W. Edwards Deming
- "You can't manage what you don't measure."

Thomas S. Monson
- "When performance is measured, performance improves."

W. Edwards Deming
- "If you can't describe what you are doing as a process, you don't know what you're doing."

30

Always Do Your Absolute Best!

Jerry's Tips:

- Always give 100% effort and enthusiasm to think, plan and take whatever action is required to achieve your goals and it will produce a tidal wave of positive attitude and unstoppable confidence that will propel you forward in life.

- When you are working on any task always push yourself to do a little more before stopping to take a break or end for the day. By getting in the habit to always do this you will build your mental strength and get you closer to achieving your goal. This is similar to doing one more repetition of lifting weights after a good workout to build your physical strength.

- Be a high performing person.

- The successful mindset is to focus 100% of your energies to be the best you can be. Excellent people strive to excel at whatever they do.

- Whether you are an employee or run your own business, to be successful you need to stand out from your competition, and the person who stands out is the person who consistently produces excellent results by giving their best effort to accomplish their goal.

- Nothing catches a more favorable eye of an employer or a customer than a person who gives 100% effort and achieves the goal of the employer or customer.

- We expect firemen, police and life guards to exert 100% effort to 'rescue' us, shouldn't we expect at least that much effort from 'ourselves' to rescue us from an unsuccessful life and create a successful life?

THE SUCCESS FORMULA FOR PERSONAL GROWTH

Andrew Carnegie
- "The average person puts only 25% of his energy and ability into his work. The world takes off its hat to those who put in more than 50% of their capacity, and stands on its head for those few and far between souls who devote 100%."

Arnold Palmer
- "Always make a total effort, even when the odds are against you."

Bob Cousy
- "Do your best when no one is looking. If you do that, then you can be successful in anything that you put your mind to."

Booker T. Washington
- "Any man's life will be filled with constant and unexpected encouragement if he makes up his mind to do his level best each day."

General George S. Patton
- "If a man does his best, what else is there?"

- "Always do more than is required of you."

Jim Collins
- "Good is the Enemy of Great."

Jim Rohn
- "Be the best you can be."

John Wooden
- "Do your best everyday. Live each day as if it's your Masterpiece."

Larry Bird
- "I've got a theory that if you give 100% all of the time, somehow things will work out in the end."

Les Brown
- "You cannot be excellent on Monday, Tuesday and Wednesday and take Thursday and Friday off. You must be excellent 'all' of the time."

Always Do Your Absolute Best!

Mary Lou Retton
"As simple as it sounds, we all must try to be the best person we can: by making the best choices, by making the most of the talents we've been given."

Og Mandino
"Always do your best. What you plant now, you will harvest later."

"Always render more and better service than is expected of you, no matter what your task may be."

Oprah Winfrey
"My philosophy is that not only are you responsible for your life, but doing the best at this moment puts you in the best place for the next moment."

Orison Swett Marden
"Never be satisfied with 'fairly good,' 'pretty good,' 'good enough.' Accept nothing short of your best."

P. T. Barnum
"Whatever you do, do it with all your might. Work at it, early and late, in season and out of season, not leaving a stone unturned, and never deferring for a single hour that which can be done just as well now."

Smiley Blanton
"All of us attain the greatest success and happiness possible in this life whenever we use our native capacities to their fullest extent."

Tony Robbins
"You can't succeed by being good. That's what you get paid for. You can't succeed by being excellent. That's what you are expected to do. You can only succeed by being outstanding."

Thomas Jefferson
"Whenever you do a thing, act as if all the world were watching."

Tyra Banks
"I'm competitive with myself. I always try to push past my own borders."

Vince Lombardi
- "There's only one way to succeed in anything, and that is to give it everything. I do, and I demand that my players do."

- "If you'll not settle for anything less than your best, you will be amazed at what you can accomplish in your life."

31

Be Enthusiastic About Everything You Do!

Jerry's Tips:

- Enthusiasm lights your fire and the fire of those around you.

- People enjoy being around enthusiastic people.

- Enthusiasm produces creativity that overcomes obstacles and solves problems.

- Enthusiasm produces results.

- You must be enthusiastic, inspired and motivated to truly inspire and motivate someone else.

- Enthusiasm turns ordinary people and results into extraordinary people and results.

- To increase your enthusiasm think about your goals everyday, and the benefits you will achieve, and how good you will feel when you accomplish them.

Charles Schwab
- "A man can succeed at almost anything for which he has unlimited enthusiasm."

Dale Carnegie
- "Act enthusiastic and you will be enthusiastic."

- "Today's life is the only life you are sure of. Make the most of today. Get interested in something. Shake yourself awake. Develop a hobby. Let the winds of enthusiasm sweep through you. Live today with gusto."

David J. Schwartz
- "Enthusiasm can make things 1,100 percent better."

- "Results come in proportion to enthusiasm applied."

- "How does one develop enthusiasm? Build in yourself an optimistic, progressive glow, a feeling that this is great and I'm 100 percent for it."

- "You are what you think. Think enthusiasm and you'll be enthusiastic."

Earl Nightingale
- "Creativity is a natural extension of our enthusiasm."

- "The key that unlocks energy is desire. It's also the key to a long and interesting life. If we expect to create any drive, any real force within ourselves, we have to get excited."

Norman Vincent Peale
- "There is a real magic in enthusiasm. It spells the difference between mediocrity and accomplishment."

- "Fill the day with enthusiasm. Give the day all you've got and it will give you all its got, which will be plenty."

Og Mandino
- "Every memorable act in the history of the world is a triumph of enthusiasm. Nothing great was ever achieved without it because it gives any challenge or any occupation, no matter how frightening or difficult, a new meaning. Without enthusiasm you are doomed to a life of mediocrity but with it you can accomplish miracles."

Pat Croce
- "Wear your enthusiasm on your sleeve."

BE ENTHUSIASTIC ABOUT EVERYTHING YOU DO!

Pele
- "Enthusiasm is everything. It must be taut and vibrating like a guitar string."

Ralph Waldo Emerson
- "Nothing great was ever achieved without enthusiasm."

32

Be Proactive, Take Initiative, Be A Go-Getter

Jerry's Tips:

- Initiative, being a self-starter, is taking the time to think or act to accomplish something worthwhile without someone asking you to do so.

- No person ever achieved success by waiting for someone to hand it to them. Successful people decide they want something and take action to get it. If you seek you will find. Get going -- Now!

- Be an initiator, someone who makes things happen. Not someone who has things happen to them.

- Seek to be active not reactive.

- Do what you need to do without being told.

- Create your own successful future.

- If you encounter setbacks or a door closes in your life don't waste time dwelling on what was, take action and create your next success.

- If you want to achieve something important you must get out there and go for it. Success won't come to you while you're lying down.

Anonymous

- "Some people make things happen, some watch things happen, while others wonder what has happened."

- "Success comes to the person who does today what you were thinking about doing tomorrow."

BE PROACTIVE, TAKE INITIATIVE, BE A GO-GETTER

- "Do it now. You become successful the moment you start moving toward a worthwhile goal."

- "Initiative is key. Anybody who wants to be somebody is going to work as hard as they can to fulfill that dream."

- "Prolonged idleness paralyzes initiative."

Anna Pavlova
- "Success depends in a very large measure upon individual initiative and exertion, and cannot be achieved except by a dint of hard work."

Bruce Lee
- "To hell with circumstances; I create opportunities."

Charles Gow
- "Notice carefully that sound judgment must precede the exercise of initiative."

Francis Bacon
- "A wise man will make more opportunities than he finds."

General George S. Patton
- "A good idea today is better than a perfect idea tomorrow."

George Bernard Shaw
- "People are always blaming their circumstances for what they are. I don't believe in circumstances. The people who get on in this world are the people who get up and look for the circumstances they want, and if they can't find them, make them."

Harry Browne
- "The important thing is to concentrate upon what you can do - by yourself, upon your own initiative."

Jim Rohn
- "Without a sense of urgency, desire loses its value."

Louis D. Brandeis
- "Organisation can never be a substitute for initiative and for judgement."

THE SUCCESS FORMULA FOR PERSONAL GROWTH

Dr. Maxwell Maltz
- "You are opportunity, and you must knock on the door leading to your destiny."

Tony Robbins
- "Success comes from taking the initiative and following up... persisting..."

Victor Hugo
- "Initiative is doing the right thing without being told."

33

Take Calculated Risks

Jerry's Tips:

- One of the biggest risks in life is to never take a calculated risk to achieve something you want.

- It is not written anywhere that always playing it safe leads to success.

- Taking a calculated risk does not mean to be foolish. Take smart risks.

- When you take a calculated risk make sure you know all of the risks and the likelihood you can succeed.

- Never risk everything you have unless you have no other choice.

Charles Lindbergh
- "I don't believe in taking foolish chances, but nothing can be accomplished without taking any chance at all."

Dale Carnegie
- "The man who goes farthest is generally the one who is willing to do and dare."

- "Take a chance! All life is a chance."

- "The sure-thing boat never gets far from shore."

Dr. Maxwell Maltz
- "Often the difference between a successful person and a failure is not that one has better abilities or ideas, but the courage that one has to bet on one's ideas, to take a calculated risk -- and to act."

THE SUCCESS FORMULA FOR PERSONAL GROWTH

Earl Nightingale
- "Wherever there is danger, there lurks opportunity; whenever there is opportunity, there lurks danger. The two are inseparable. They go together."

- "You can measure opportunity with the same yardstick that measures the risk involved. They go together."

General George S. Patton
- "Take calculated risks. That is quite different from being rash."

James Allen
- "Whether you be man or woman you will never do anything in this world without courage. It is the greatest quality of the mind next to honor."

Joseph Heller
- "Opportunity always involves some risk. You can't steal second base and keep your foot on first!"

Muhammad Ali
- "He who is not courageous enough to take risks will accomplish nothing in life."

Oprah Winfrey
- "I believe that one of life's greatest risks is never daring to risk."

Robert F. Kennedy
- "Only those who dare to fail greatly can ever achieve greatly."

Robert Kiyosaki
- "In the real world outside of academics, something more than just good grades is required. I have heard it called 'guts,' 'chutzpah,' 'balls,' 'audacity,' bravado,' 'cunning,' 'daring,' 'tenacity,' and 'brilliance.' This factor, whatever it is labeled, ultimately decides one's future much more than school grades." Success demands action."

Steven Covey
- "The greatest risk is the risk of riskless living."

Will Rogers
- "Why not go out on a limb? That's where the fruit is."

TAKE CALCULATED RISKS

William B. Sprague

- "You will never do anything in this world without courage. It is the greatest quality of the mind next to honor."

34

Believe In Yourself!
Self-Respect, Self-Esteem,
Self-Confidence

Jerry's Tips:

- Having Self-Respect and Self-Esteem means you have unshakeable personal beliefs that:

    1. You're a good person regardless of what other people may think of you,

    2. You are comfortable in your own skin,

    3. You are worthy of success,

    4. You are an important person and worthy of respect and consideration,

    5. You can influence other people, and

    6. You trust and have faith in your abilities to meet, and overcome any challenge or setback to achieve your desired goals.

- Believe in yourself and believe you can achieve your goals, and you will!

- To accomplish anything significant in life you must always believe you can do it and believe you deserve it.

- What is behind you or ahead of you is far less important than what is inside of you.

- Believing in your own self-worth is priceless.

- Hold yourself in high regard and your abilities will shine.

BELIEVE IN YOURSELF!
SELF-RESPECT, SELF-ESTEEM, SELF-CONFIDENCE

- Self-Confidence is a rock solid feeling of certainty and trust that you can achieve what you want and handle specific skills and circumstances.

- Believe that you are important. Feel important.

- Be confident – not arrogant; confidence is believing in your abilities and trusting yourself that you can handle any situation. Arrogance is thinking you are better than someone else.

- Whatever confidence you believe and display in yourself, you should also believe exists in everyone you meet. Then they won't think you're arrogant, they will respect you.

- Always believe that you can solve any problem. The solution is out there. You know you just have to find it.

- To be confident, focus on your desired outcome not on the difficulty to get there.

- To build confidence set small goals and achieve them. Achieving any goal builds confidence. Setting goals and achieving them is the #1 way to develop confidence.

- Intensely practice imagining yourself as confident and you will become confident.

- Act confident and you will become confident.

- Try to limit your exposure to advertisements. Their purpose is to make you feel dissatisfied, that you have unmet needs and that only by having whatever they are pushing will you feel good and be respected by other people.

- To improve your self-esteem and be comfortable in your own skin realize that your life is a priceless gift to yourself and your loved ones and friends.

THE SUCCESS FORMULA FOR PERSONAL GROWTH

Abraham Lincoln
- "I am not bothered by what others said about me as long as I know they did not speak the truth."

Anonymous
- "It's not who you are that holds you back, it's who you think you're not."

- "Nine out of ten people who change their minds are wrong the second time too."

- "If you want to be respected, you must respect yourself."

Baltasar Gracian
- "Attempt easy tasks as if they were difficult, and difficult as if they were easy; in the one case that confidence may not fall asleep, in the other that it may not be dismayed."

Bob Proctor
- "Science and psychology have isolated the one prime cause for success or failure in life. It is the hidden self-image you have of yourself."

Bruce Barton
- "Nothing splendid has ever been achieved except by those who dared believe that something inside of them was superior to circumstance."

Brian Tracy
- "The person we believe ourselves to be will always act in a manner consistent with our self-image."

- "The way you give your name to others is a measure of how much you like and respect yourself."

- "Confidence is a habit that can be developed by acting as if you already had the confidence you desire to have."

Cavett Robert
- "The only chains and shackles that prevent any of us from realizing our life's dreams are those we ourselves forge in the fires of doubt and hammer out on the anvil of lack of belief in what we say or do."

BELIEVE IN YOURSELF!
SELF-RESPECT, SELF-ESTEEM, SELF-CONFIDENCE

David J. Schwartz

- "You must feel important to succeed."

- "Never sell yourself short."

- "Look important - it helps you think important."

- "Your appearance 'talks.' Be sure it says positive things about you. Never leave home without feeling certain you look like the kind of person you want to be."

- "The most honest advertisement ever appearing in print is 'Dress Right. You Can't Afford Not To!' "

- "Your appearance is the first basis for evaluation other people have. And first impressions last, out of all proportion to the time it takes to form them."

- "To have a great wardrobe pay twice as much and buy half as many."

- "Your appearance talks to you and it talks to others. Make certain it says, "Here is a person who has self-respect. He's important. Treat him that way."

- "You owe it to others, but, more important, you owe it to yourself - to look your best."

- "You are what you think you are. If your appearance makes you think you're inferior, you are inferior. If it makes you think small, you are small. Look your best and you will think and act your best."

- "To think confidently, act confidently... Act the way you want to feel."

- "All confidence is acquired, developed. No one is born with confidence. Those people you know who radiate confidence, who have conquered worry, who are at ease everywhere and all the time, acquired their confidence, every bit of it. I can too."

THE SUCCESS FORMULA FOR PERSONAL GROWTH

- "Believe Big. The size of your success is determined by the size of your belief. Think little goals and expect little achievements. Think big goals and win big success. Remember this, too! Big ideas and big plans are often easier -- certainly no more difficult - than small ideas and small plans."

- "Remind yourself regularly that you are better than you think you are. Successful people are not superhuman. Success does not require a super-intellect. Nor is there anything mystical about success. And success isn't based on luck. Successful people are just ordinary folks who have developed belief in themselves and what they do."

James W. Newman
- "You are an extremely valuable, worthwhile, significant person even though your present circumstances may have you feeling otherwise."

Dr. Joyce Brothers
- "Success is a state of mind. If you want success, start thinking of yourself as a success."

Dr. Robert H. Schuller
- "Every achiever that I have ever met says, 'My life turned around when I began to believe in me.'"

Fyodor Dostoyevsky
- "If you want to be respected by others the great thing is to respect yourself. Only by that, only by self-respect will you compel others to respect you."

Helen Keller
- "Never bend your head. Always hold it high. Look the world straight in the face."

Henry Ford
- "Whether you believe you can do a thing or not, you're right."

Henry David Thoreau
- "What a man thinks of himself - that is which determines, or rather indicates his fate."

John McEnroe
- "I think it's the mark of a great player to be confident in tough situations."

BELIEVE IN YOURSELF!
SELF-RESPECT, SELF-ESTEEM, SELF-CONFIDENCE

Judith M. Bardwick
- "Real confidence comes from knowing and accepting yourself - your strengths and your limitations - in contrast to depending on confirmation from others."

Kenneth Cole
- "How you see yourself is the way you'll end up being."

Les Brown
- "Love yourself unconditionally, just as you love those closest to you despite their faults."

Mohandas Gandhi
- "Man often becomes what he believes himself to be. If I keep on saying to myself that I cannot do a certain thing, it is possible that I may end by really becoming incapable of doing it. On the contrary, if I shall have the belief that I can do it, I shall surely acquire the capacity to do it, even if I may not have it at the beginning."

Marcus Garvey
- "If you have no confidence in yourself, you are twice defeated in the race of life. With confidence, you have won even before you have started."

Mark Twain
- "A man cannot be comfortable without his own approval."

- "The worst loneliness is to not be comfortable with yourself."

- "A man cannot be comfortable without his own approval. There is nothing more satisfying than that sense of being completely 'at home' in your own skin. When you achieve that as a natural state of 'being', then you can finally look beyond yourself and fully contribute all your talents to the world."

Dr. Maxwell Maltz
- "Low self esteem is like driving through life with your hand brake on."

- "Real self esteem is not derived from the great things you've done, the things you won, the mark you've made - but an appreciation of yourself for what you are."

- "Accept yourself as you are. Otherwise you will never see opportunity. You will not feel free to move toward it; you will feel you are not deserving."

Mohandas Gandhi
- "If I have the belief that I can do it, I shall surely acquire the capacity to do it even if I may not have it at the beginning."

Morrie Schwartz
- "So many of us are too hard on ourselves for what we didn't accomplish or what we should have done. The first step is to forgive yourself for all the things you didn't do that you should have, and all the things that you did do that you shouldn't have."

Muhammad Ali
- "To be a great champion you must believe you are the best. If you're not, pretend you are."

Nathaniel Branden
- "Of all the judgments we pass in life, none is more important than the judgment we pass on ourselves."

Nido Qubein
- "If you believe you can, and believe it strongly enough, you'll be amazed at what you can do."

Norman Vincent Peale
- "People become really quite remarkable when they start thinking that they can do things. When they believe in themselves they have the first secret of success."

- "Formulate and stamp indelibly on your mind a mental picture of yourself as succeeding. Hold this picture tenaciously. Never permit it to fade. Your mind will seek to develop the picture...Do not build up obstacles in your imagination."

- "Reject defeat, banish obstacles."

Og Mandino
- "Today I will be master of my emotions.
  If I feel depressed I will sing.
  If I feel sad I will laugh.
  If I feel ill I will double my labor.
  If I feel fear I will plunge ahead.

BELIEVE IN YOURSELF!
SELF-RESPECT, SELF-ESTEEM, SELF-CONFIDENCE

If I feel inferior I will wear new garments.
If I feel uncertain I will raise my voice.
If I feel poverty I will think of wealth to come.
If I feel incompetent I will remember past success.
If I feel insignificant I will remember my goals."

Ralph Waldo Emerson
"What lies behind us and what lies before us are tiny matters compared to what lies within us."

Robert Collier
"Your chances of success in any undertaking can always be measured by your belief in yourself."

Samuel Smiles
"Self-respect is the noblest garment with which a man may clothe himself; the most elevating feeling with which the mind can be inspired."

Stan Smith
"Experience tells you what to do; confidence allows you to do it."

Steven Covey
"Our ultimate freedom is the right and power to decide how anybody or anything outside ourselves will affect us."

Theodore Roosevelt
"Whenever you are asked if you can do a job, tell 'em 'Certainly I can!' and get busy and find out how to do it."

Thomas Carlyle
"Nothing builds self-esteem and self-confidence like accomplishment."

Vince Lombardi
"Confidence is contagious and so is lack of confidence."

Virgil
"They can do all because they think they can."

THE SUCCESS FORMULA FOR PERSONAL GROWTH

Wally (Famous) Amos
- "It's so important to believe in yourself. Believe that you can do it, under any circumstances. Because if you believe you can, then you really will. That belief just keeps you searching for the answers, and then pretty soon you get it."

Wayne Dyer
- "Self-worth comes from one thing - thinking that you are worthy."

Zig Ziglar
- "When you look good you feel more confident and competent."

- "If you dress sharp, you feel sharp."

- "When you look sharp, you feel sharp, and then that makes you sharp."

- "When you make up and dress up your chances of going up are definitely going to be improved."

- "When your image improves, your performance improves."

- "If you don't see yourself as a winner, then you cannot perform as a winner."

35

Have A Positive Attitude, Be Optimistic

Jerry's Tips:

- Maintain positive thoughts, positive attitudes and positive actions throughout the day and you will have a positive day.

- How far you can go and succeed tomorrow is determined by your attitude today.

- Having a positive attitude enables you to do everything you do better than if you have a negative attitude.

- Think that you died and just came back to life. Think how great you would feel; you'd be extremely happy, excited, energized, eager to enjoy life and you would see the best in everything. When you have a positive attitude like that you will want to set goals and work hard to achieve them to be successful. This is the attitude you should always maintain.

- Don't let other people destroy your positive attitude. When other people gossip about something depressing or negative that really has no impact to your life or theirs and they are on Channel N (Negative), you should politely change your conversation topic to Channel P (Positive), or say you have to leave to do something else.

- Every night before you go to sleep and when you wake up in the morning fill your mind with thoughts that you are very lucky and grateful for all of the things you have and tell yourself that you know that you will have a great day and will be successful working on your goals.

THE SUCCESS FORMULA FOR PERSONAL GROWTH

- Having a positive attitude is not something you do once in a while. Like car headlights, when driving at night on an unlit road, your positive attitude must always be turned on bright or you will only see darkness.

- Whenever you catch yourself thinking about worry, doubt or fear, quickly change your thoughts and think about something in your life that you are very proud of and remind yourself that you have tremendous abilities and can accomplish anything you decide to do.

Anonymous
- "The winner says, 'It may be difficult, but it is possible.' The loser says, 'It may be possible, but it is too difficult.'"

Bill Clinton
- "Pessimism is an excuse for not trying and a guarantee to a personal failure."

Bob Boshnack
- "The longer I live, the more I realize the impact of a positive mental attitude on life. PMA, as it is called, is to me more important than the past, than education, than money, than circumstances, than failures, than successes, than what other people think or say or do. It is more important than appearance, giftedness, or skill. It will make or break a company...a church...a home or a person."

Charles R. Swindoll
- "We cannot change our past...we cannot change the fact that people will act in a certain way. We cannot change the inevitable. The only thing we can do is play on the one string we have, and that is our attitude... I am convinced that life is 10% what happens to me and 90% how I react to it. And so it is with you. We are in charge of our attitudes."

Clint Eastwood
- "I don't believe in pessimism. If something doesn't come up the way you want, forge ahead. If you think it's going to rain, it will."

David J. Schwartz
- "Attitudes are more important than intelligence."

HAVE A POSITIVE ATTITUDE
BE OPTIMISITC

Dwight D. Eisenhower
"Pessimism never won any battle."

Earl Nightingale
"Our environment, the world in which we live and work, is a mirror of our attitudes and expectations."

Eddie Rickenbacker
"Think positively and masterfully, with confidence and faith, and life becomes more secure, more fraught with action, richer in achievement and experience."

Franklin D. Roosevelt
"The only limit to our realization of tomorrow will be our doubts of today."

General Colin Powell
"Perpetual optimism is a force multiplier."

Harry S. Truman
"A pessimist is one who makes difficulties of his opportunities and an optimist is one who makes opportunities of his difficulties."

Helen Keller
"Optimism is the faith that leads to achievement. Nothing can be done without hope and confidence."

"No pessimist ever discovered the secret of the stars or sailed to an uncharted land or opened a new heaven to the human spirit."

Japanese Proverb
"If you look up, there are no limits."

Lou Holtz
"Ability is what you're capable of doing...Motivation determines what you do...Attitude determines how well you do it."

Mark Twain
"There is nothing sadder than a young pessimist."

THE SUCCESS FORMULA FOR PERSONAL GROWTH

Og Mandino
- "Forget the happenings of the day that is gone, whether they were good or bad, and greet the new sun with confidence that this will be the best day of your life."

Oprah Winfrey
- "The greatest discovery of all time is that a person can change his future by merely changing his attitude."

Oscar Wilde
- "A pessimist is somebody who complains about the noise when opportunity knocks."

Pat Croce
- "Research proves that a positive attitude trends toward success. Dr, Martin Seligman at the University of Pa. studied students, athletes, and insurance salesmen, and concluded that in almost every case, the modestly-talented optimist – like you know who - outperformed the highly-talented pessimist. Which are you?"

Pat Riley
- "Great effort springs naturally from great attitude."

- "Shoulda, coulda, and woulda won't get it done. In attacking adversity, only a positive attitude, alertness, and regrouping to basics can launch a comeback."

Rene Descartes
- "An optimist may see a light where there is none, but why must the pessimist always run to blow it out?"

Richard M. DeVos
- "Few things in the world are more powerful than a positive push. A smile. A world of optimism and hope. A 'you can do it' when things are tough."

Thomas Jefferson
- "Nothing can stop the man with the right mental attitude from achieving his goal; nothing on earth can help the man with the wrong attitude."

HAVE A POSITIVE ATTITUDE
BE OPTIMISITC

Venus Williams
- "Some people say that I have an attitude - Maybe I do. But I think that you have to. You have to believe in yourself when no one else does - that makes you a winner right there."

W. Clement Stone
- "There is very little difference in people, but that little difference makes a big difference. The little difference is attitude."

William James
- "It is our attitude at the beginning of a difficult task which, more than anything else, will affect its successful outcome."

Winston Churchill
- "Attitude is a little thing that makes a big difference."

- "A pessimist sees the difficulty in every opportunity; an optimist sees the opportunity in every difficulty."

Zig Ziglar
- "Positive thinking will let you do everything better than negative thinking will."

- "Your attitude, not your aptitude, will determine your altitude."

- "An optimist is someone who goes after Moby Dick in a rowboat and takes the tartar sauce with him."

36

Never Quit!

Be Mentally Tough, Determined, Patient, Tenacious, Persistent And Be Relentlessly Resourceful

Jerry's Tips:

- Everything that's ever been accomplished was done by a human being. And what are you? That's right, a human being. You can achieve anything you want so long as you have the determination and tenacity to get off your butt and do what it takes to accomplish it.

- Attack your goals each day with the mindset that you are relentlessly advancing step by step to complete them and will overcome all obstacles.

- Desire what you want to achieve with every fiber of your being, and with unshakable belief that you will accomplish it – and You Will!

- Have an Iron Will.

- Willpower is the unflinching purpose to see a task through to completion.

- Persistence breaks down resistance.

- Hard work towards achieving your goals does not take something out of you. It puts something in… The mindset that you can achieve whatever you want to!

- Think big thoughts that give you strength and make you resilient.

- Be unstoppable, be tenacious, be indomitable!

NEVER QUIT!
BE MENTALLY TOUGH, DETERMINED, PATIENT, TENACIOUS, PERSISTENT AND BE RELENTLESSLY RESOURCEFUL

- The difference between a loser and a winner is very simple: a loser quits when things get tough and a winner never quits. Learn this lesson and live it, and you will be successful.

- Resourcefulness is the ability to do a lot with a little.

- Resourcefulness is the ability to act effectively or imaginatively, especially in difficult situations.

- Resourceful people can make things happen when the chips are down.

- Resourcefulness develops in response to scarcity and the need to be an active, inquisitive problem solver.

- Being resourceful means knowing how to get the information and results you want.

- Resourcefulness = Necessity + Creativity + Intelligence + Efficiency + Persistence.

- Resourcefulness is figuring out and taking action to get things done when the path is not clear. It is focusing on solutions rather than problems.

- A resourceful person steps up to the plate and solves unexpected problems.

Abraham Lincoln
- "You can have anything you want, if you want it badly enough. You can be anything you want to be, do anything you set out to accomplish if you hold to that desire with singleness of purpose."

Adlai E. Stevenson
- "On the plains of hesitation lie the blackened bones of countless millions who at the dawn of victory lay down to rest, and in resting died."

THE SUCCESS FORMULA FOR PERSONAL GROWTH

Albert Einstein
- "It's not that I'm so smart, it's just that I stay with problems longer."

Andy Munthe
- "A shot glass of desire is greater than a pitcher of talent."

Anonymous
- "Where there's a will there's a way."

- "Rome wasn't built in a day."

- "You haven't failed till you quit trying."

- "Failure is the path of least persistence."

Arnold Palmer
- "I've always made a total effort, even when the odds seemed entirely against me. I never quit trying; I never felt that I didn't have a chance to win."

Babe Ruth
- "What do I think about when I strike out? I think about hitting home runs."

Benjamin Disraeli
- "A human being with a settled purpose must accomplish it, and nothing can resist a will that will stake even existence for its fulfillment."

- "Through perseverance many people win success out of what seemed destined to be certain failure."

Benjamin Franklin
- "Energy and persistence conquer all things."

Bill Cosby
- "In order to succeed, your desire for success must be greater than your fear of failure."

NEVER QUIT!
BE MENTALLY TOUGH, DETERMINED, PATIENT, TENACIOUS, PERSISTENT AND BE RELENTLESSLY RESOURCEFUL

Bjorn Borg
- "My greatest point is my persistence. I never give up in a match. However down I am, I fight until the last ball. My list of matches shows that I have turned a great many so-called irretrievable defeats into victories."

Brian Tracy
- "The only real limitation on your abilities is the level of your desires. If you want it badly enough, there are no limits on what you can achieve."

Calvin Coolidge
- "Nothing in the world can take the place of persistence. Talent will not; nothing is more common than unsuccessful men with talent. Genius will not; unsuccessful genius is almost a proverb. Education will not; the world is full of educated derelicts. Persistence and determination alone are omnipotent. The slogan; 'press on', has solved and will solve the problems of the human race."

Chuck Norris
- "A lot of people give up just before they're about to make it. You know, you never know when that next obstacle is going to be the last one."

Confucius
- "Our greatest glory is not in never falling, but in rising every time we fall."

Conrad Hilton
- "Success seems to be connected with action. Successful people keep moving. They make mistakes but they never quit."

Dale Carnegie
- "Most of the important things in the world have been accomplished by people who have kept on trying when there seemed to be no hope at all."

David Sarnoff
- "The will to persevere is often the difference between failure and success."

THE SUCCESS FORMULA FOR PERSONAL GROWTH

Donald Trump

"When it comes to success you cannot give up. You have to keep going and moving forward, no matter what is happening around you or to you. It's a form of positive thinking that is very powerful. A word that comes to mind as a result of this approach is 'indomitable.' I overcame some great setbacks just by being obstinate. I refused to give in or give up. To me, that's integrity of purpose that cannot be defeated or interfered with to any significant level. Being steadfast in your intentions can reap great results.

The other word I like to think of along with indomitable is 'tenacious.' In a way, they are almost interchangeable when it comes to business. Being tenacious will make you indomitable in the long run. The old tortoise versus the hare story still prevails."

"Sometimes you just have to be tough. I use the example of a brick wall. Is there a brick wall getting in your way? Fine. That happens. But you have a choice. You can walk away from the wall. You can go over the wall. You can go under the wall. You can go around the wall. You can also obliterate the wall. In other words, don't let anything get in your way. Get a balance, and then let the positive outdistance the negative."

"I was relentless, even in the face of total lack of encouragement, because much more often than you'd think, sheer persistence is the difference between success and failure."

Eddie Robinson

"The will to win, the desire to succeed, the urge to reach your full potential... these are the keys that will unlock the door to personal excellence."

English Proverb

"Where there's a will, there is a way."

Frank Marino

(Question from an Interviewer) Do you think music can be taught or learned by anyone if they try, or do you have to be born with a certain natural talent?

NEVER QUIT!
BE MENTALLY TOUGH, DETERMINED, PATIENT, TENACIOUS, PERSISTENT AND BE RELENTLESSLY RESOURCEFUL

- "I think it can be taught and learned, but it's not talent you need to be gifted with, but desire. If anyone really desires to do something, they will become a master of it, no doubt about it. I mean, this is supposing of course that there is no physical reason stopping them, but that aside, anyone can master anything they really want to do....and I truly believe that, it's not just lip-service or a bullshit cliché answer."

Franklin D. Roosevelt
- "When you get to the end of your rope, tie a knot and hang on."

Frederick Douglass
- "Men may not get all they pay for in this world, but they must certainly pay for all they get."

Gale Sayers
- "I learned that if you want to make it bad enough, no matter how bad it is, you can make it."

General George S. Patton
- "Success is how high you bounce when you hit bottom."

George Lucas
- "Working hard is very important. You're not going to get anywhere without working extremely hard."

H. Jackson Brown, Jr.
- "In the confrontation between the stream and the rock, the stream always, wins - not through strength but by perseverance."

Hannibal
- "We will either find a way, or make one!"

Hank Aaron
- "My motto was always to keep swinging. Whether I was in a slump or feeling badly or having trouble off the field, the only thing to do was keep swinging."

Harriet Beecher Stowe
- "When you get into a tight place and everything goes against you, till it seems as though you could not hang on a minute longer, never give up then, for that is just the place and time that the tide will turn."

Helen Keller
- "We can do anything we want to do if we stick to it long enough."

Henry Ford
- "Obstacles are those frightful things you see when you take your eyes off the goal."

Henry Wadsworth Longfellow
- "Perseverance is a great element of success. If you only knock long enough and loud enough at the gate, you are sure to wake up somebody."

Isaac Newton
- "If I have ever made any valuable discoveries, it has been owing more to patient attention, than to any other talent."

Jack Dempsey
- "A champion is someone who gets up even when he can't."

Jacob A. Riis
- "Look at a stone cutter hammering away at his rock, perhaps a hundred times without as much as a crack showing in it. Yet at the hundred-and-first blow it will split in two, and I know it was not the last blow that did it, but all that had gone before."

James Allen
- "He who would accomplish little must sacrifice little; he who would achieve much must sacrifice much; he who would attain highly must sacrifice greatly."
- "In all human affairs there are efforts, and there are results, and the strength of the effort is the measure of the result."

James J. Corbett
- "You become a champion by fighting one more round. When things are tough, you fight one more round."

NEVER QUIT!
BE MENTALLY TOUGH, DETERMINED, PATIENT, TENACIOUS, PERSISTENT AND BE RELENTLESSLY RESOURCEFUL

Jerry West
- "You can't get much done in life if you only work on the days when you feel good."

Jesse Owens
- "We all have dreams. But in order to make dreams come into reality, it takes an awful lot of determination, dedication, self-discipline, and effort."

Jim Collins
- "You must maintain unwavering faith that you can and will prevail in the end, regardless of the difficulties, and at the same time, have the discipline to confront the most brutal facts of your current reality, whatever they might be."

Jim Rohn
- "When you know what you want and you want it badly enough, you'll find a way to get it."

John Quincy Adams
- "Patience and perseverance have a magical effect before which difficulties disappear and obstacles vanish."

John McEnroe
- "What is the single most important quality in a tennis champion? I would have to say desire, staying in there and winning matches when you are not playing that well."

John D. Rockefeller, Jr.
- "I do not think there is any other quality so essential to success of any kind as the quality of perseverance. It overcomes almost everything…"

Lee Iacocca
- "You've got to say, 'I think that if I keep working at this and want it badly enough I can have it.' It's called perseverance."

Les Brown
- Anytime you suffer a setback or disappointment, put your head down and plow ahead."

- "When life knocks you down, try to land on your back. Because if you can look up, you can get up. Let your reason get you back up."

- "You gotta be hungry!"

Louis Pasteur
- "Let me tell you the secret that has led me to my goal. My strength lies solely in my tenacity."

Marie Curie
- "Life is not easy for any of us. But what of that? We must have perseverance and above all confidence in ourselves. We must believe that we are gifted for something and that this thing must be attained."

Mario Andretti
- "Desire is the key to motivation, but it's the determination and commitment to an unrelenting pursuit of your goal -- a commitment to excellence – that will enable you to attain the success you seek."

Mark Twain
- "It's not the size of the dog in the fight, it's the size of the fight in the dog."

Martin Luther King, Jr.
- "The true measure of a man is not how he behaves in moments of comfort and convenience but how he stands at times of controversy and challenges."

Michael Jordan
- "Obstacles don't have to stop you. If you run into a wall, don't turn around and give up. Figure out how to climb it, go through it, or work around it."

Michael Phelps
- "I think that everything is possible as long as you put your mind to it and you put the work and time into it. I think your mind really controls everything."

Mike Ditka
- "If you are determined enough and willing to pay the price, you can get it done."

- "You're never a loser until you quit trying."

Never Quit!
Be mentally tough, determined, patient, tenacious, persistent and be relentlessly resourceful

- "If things came easy, then everybody would be great at what they did, let's face it."

Miyamoto Musashi
- "'Crossing at a ford' means, for example, crossing the sea at a strait, or crossing over a hundred miles of broad sea at a crossing place. I believe this 'crossing at a ford' occurs often in a man's lifetime. It means setting sail even though your friends stay in harbour, knowing the route, knowing the soundness of your ship and the favour of the day. When all the conditions are met, and there is perhaps a favourable wind, or a tailwind, then set sail. If the wind changes within a few miles of your destination, you must row across the remaining distance without sail. If you attain this spirit, it applies to everyday life. You must always think of crossing at a ford."

Napoleon Hill
- "A quitter never wins and a winner never quits."

- "Patience, persistence and perspiration make an unbeatable combination for success."

- "No man is ever whipped until he quits in his own mind."

- "There is one quality that one must possess to win, and that is definiteness of purpose, the knowledge of what one wants, and a burning desire to possess it."

- "Before success comes in any man's life he is sure to meet with much temporary defeat and, perhaps, some failures. When defeat overtakes a man, the easiest and most logical thing to do is to quit. That is exactly what the majority of men do."

Newt Gingrich
- "Perseverance is the hard work you do after you get tired of doing the hard work you already did."

Og Mandino
- "If you persist long enough you will win."

- "Failure will never overtake me if my determination to succeed is strong enough."

- "I will persist until I succeed."

- "I will never consider defeat and I will remove from my vocabulary such words and phrases as quit, cannot, unable, impossible, out of the question, improbable, failure, unworkable, hopeless, and retreat."

Pat Croce
- "Instill the habit of persistence and you will achieve the habit of success."

Dr. Robert H. Schuller
- "Tough times never last, but tough people do."

Roger Bannister
- "The man who can drive himself further once the effort gets painful is the man who will win."

Ruben Gonzalez
- "If you have a dream; your willing to go for it; and you refuse to quit; dreams do come true."

Pat Croce
- "Your IQ is not as important as your I WILL."

- "While there's a limit to the amount of knowledge you can accumulate there's no limit whatsoever to your dreams and determination."

Ralph Waldo Emerson
- "Patience and fortitude conquer all things."

Ross Perot
- "Most people give up just when they're about to achieve success. They quit on the one yard line. They give up at the last minute of the game one foot from a winning touchdown."

Samuel Johnson
- "Great works are performed not by strength but by perseverance."

Serena and Venus Williams
- "Champions don't let anything stand in their way. To make it to the top you have to stick to your goal no matter what."

NEVER QUIT!
BE MENTALLY TOUGH, DETERMINED, PATIENT, TENACIOUS, PERSISTENT AND BE RELENTLESSLY RESOURCEFUL

Saint Augustine
- "Patience is the companion of wisdom."

Thomas Edison
- "Our greatest weakness lies in giving up. The most certain way to succeed is always to try just one more time."

- "Genius is one percent inspiration and ninety-nine percent perspiration."

- "Nearly every man who develops an idea works it up to the point where it looks impossible, and then he gets discouraged. That's not the place to become discouraged."

- "Many of life's failures are men who did not realize how close they were to success when they gave up."

Thomas Fuller
- "An invincible determination can accomplish almost anything and in this lies the great distinction between great men and little men."

Tommy Lasorda
- "The difference between the impossible and the possible lies in a man's determination."

Vince Lombardi
- "The difference between a successful person and others is not a lack of strength, not a lack of knowledge, but rather a lack of will."

- "The dictionary is the only place that success comes before work. Hard work is the price we must pay for success. I think you can accomplish anything if you're willing to pay the price."

- "It's not whether you get knocked down, it's whether you get up."

- "Mental toughness is essential to success."

- "Mental toughness is many things and rather difficult to explain. Its qualities are sacrifice and self-denial. Also, most importantly, it is combined with a perfectly disciplined will that refuses to give in. It's a state of mind-you could call it character in action."

THE SUCCESS FORMULA FOR PERSONAL GROWTH

- "Winning is not everything, but wanting to win is."

W. Clement Stone
- "Success is achieved and maintained by those who try and keep trying."

- "Try, try, try, and keep on trying is the rule that must be followed to become an expert in anything."

Wayne Dyer
- "There is no scarcity of opportunity to make a living at what you love to do, there is only scarcity of resolve to make it happen."

William E. Hickson
- "If at first you don't succeed, try, try, try again."

Winston Churchill
- "Never, never, never, never, never, in nothing great or small, large or petty, never give in, except to convictions of honour and good sense. Never yield to force; never yield to the apparently overwhelming might of the enemy."

- "Continuous effort - not strength or intelligence - is the key to unlocking our potential."

- "If you're going through hell, keep going."

Zig Ziglar
- "The major difference between the big shot and the little shot is the big shot is just a little shot who kept on shooting."

37

Figure Out How To Inspire And Motivate Yourself

Jerry's Tips:

- Figure out what motivates you and why, and keep doing it until you succeed.

- Don't rely on anyone to provide your motivation; because they may not be around when you need motivation.

- A self-motivated person will always find the road to success even without a map. A person without self-motivation can't find success even if it's right in front of them.

- Remind yourself often that you can succeed – and you will.

- Self-motivation is more powerful than talent.

- Write down a list of the benefits you will get by achieving your goals and read it several times each day. This will remind you why you are working on these goals and will encourage you to do your best.

Andrew Carnegie
- "People who are unable to motivate themselves must be content with mediocrity, no matter how impressive their other talents."

Anonymous
- "Our dependency makes slaves out of us, especially if this dependency is a dependency of our self-esteem. If you need encouragement, praise, pats on the back from everybody, then you make everybody your judge."

THE SUCCESS FORMULA FOR PERSONAL GROWTH

Dale Carnegie
- "The person who seeks all their applause from outside has their happiness in another's keeping."

Jim Rohn
- "The best motivation is self-motivation. The guy says, 'I wish someone would come by and turn me on.' What if they don't show up? You've got to have a better plan for your life."

Les Brown
- "Wanting something is not enough. You must hunger for it. Your motivation must be absolutely compelling in order to overcome the obstacles that will invariably come your way."

Norman R. Augustine
- "Motivation will almost always beat mere talent."

Steven Covey
- "Motivation is a fire from within. If someone else tries to light that fire under you, chances are it will burn very briefly."

Tony Dorsett
- "To succeed you need to find something to hold on to, something to motivate you, something to inspire you."

Wayne Dyer
- "Be miserable - or motivate yourself. Whatever has to be done, it's always your choice."

Zig Ziglar
- "People often say that motivation doesn't last. Well, neither does bathing - that's why we recommend it daily."

38

Have Supportive Friends

Jerry's Tips:

- A friend is someone who encourages you and can raise your spirits and wants you to succeed.

- A friend makes life more enjoyable by spending time together on common interests.

- A friend will be honest with you about your flaws and suggest how to improve them.

- The value of a good friend is priceless. No amount of money can buy a true friend.

- To have a good friend, be a good friend.

- If you don't have a good friend figure out why and do something to find someone you can be good friends with.

- There is no shortage of people who want to be good friends with other good people. You just need to have the courage to be yourself around others.

Henry Ford
- "My best friend is the one who brings out the best in me."

Jay Leno
- "Go through your phone book, call people and ask them to drive you to the airport. The ones who will drive you are your true friends. The rest aren't bad people; they're just acquaintances."

Mark Twain
- "Really great people make you feel that you, too, can become great."

THE SUCCESS FORMULA FOR PERSONAL GROWTH

Miguel De Cervantes
- "Tell me what company thou keepst, and I'll tell thee what thou art."

Oprah Winfrey
- "Lots of people want to ride with you in the limo, but what you want is someone who will take the bus with you when the limo breaks down."

- "Surround yourself with only people who are going to lift you higher."

Walter Winchel
- "A friend is one who walks in when others walk out."

39

Avoid Unsuccessful And Unsupportive People

Jerry's Tips:

- Negative people are like two ton anchors. They weigh you down and prevent you from going anywhere.

- If you have a dream to do something don't listen to other people who tell you it can't be done if they have never attempted to do what you want to do.

- The hottest fire can be extinguished by water. In the same way, your burning desire to accomplish your goals will be extinguished if you absorb the constant complaining, laziness, pessimism, lack of self-confidence and lack of self-esteem of people around you.

David J. Schwartz
- "People who tell you it cannot be done almost always are unsuccessful people, are strictly average or mediocre at best in terms of accomplishment. The opinions of these people can be poison."

Jean Louis Etienne
- "Everything looks impossible for the people who never try anything."

Les Brown
- "If you run around with 9 losers pretty soon you'll be the 10th loser."

- "Don't let someone else's opinion of you become your reality."

Mariah Carey
- "This is for all of you out there tonight, reaching for a dream - don't ever give up! Never ever listen to anyone when they try to discourage you, because they do that, believe me!"

Mark Twain
- "Keep away from people who try to belittle your ambitions. Small people always do that, but the really great make you feel that you, too, can become great."

Vince Lombardi
- "Confidence is contagious. So is lack of confidence."

Virginia Satir
- "We must not allow other people's limited perceptions to define us."

W. Clement Stone
- "Be careful the friends you choose for you will become like them."

40

Make Decisive Decisions

Jerry's Tips:

- Making a decisive decision means to be able to quickly make a decision to do something, or not to do something, even if the choices are ambiguous and all of the facts are not yet known.

- An example of being decisive in ordinary life is that a decisive person can order a meal quickly even if the menu is very long while others sit and read the menu again and again and can't make up their mind.

- Successful people are very good at making decisive decisions. It allows them to act and do while others would only think and do nothing.

- A decisive person is not an impulsive decision maker. They do not oppose thinking through the various choices. But when they decide the time is right to make their decision they decide quickly.

- You can start to become a decisive person by making a decisive decision right now to stop being indecisive.

- Decisive people balance reason and their emotions in their decisions.

- To be decisive, be informed, get clarity, understand the problem, consider the pros and cons of alternative choices, and trust your gut to make the right decision.

Aldous Huxley
- "Facts do not cease to exist because they are ignored."

Carl Jung
- "To ask the right question is already half the solution of a problem."

- "Intuition is perception via the unconscious."

Carlos Castaneda
- "A rule of thumb for a warrior is that he makes his decisions so carefully that nothing that may happen as a result of them can surprise him, much less drain his power."

Chinese Proverb
- "A wise man makes his own decisions, an ignorant man follows public opinion. Listen to all, plucking a feather from every passing goose, but, follow no one absolutely."

Donald Trump
- "Leaders are people who can discern the inevitable and act accordingly. When people talk about business acumen, discernment is a big part of it. It's a bit like gut instinct, but a little more developed."

- "Go with your Gut."

- "I'm a great believer in asking everyone for an opinion before I make a decision. I ask I ask I ask, until I begin to get a gut feeling about something. And that's when I make a decision. I have learned much more from conducting my own random surveys than I could ever have learned from the greatest of consulting firms."

Dr. Joyce Brothers
- "Trust your hunches. They're usually based on facts filed away just below the conscious level."

Dr. Phil
- "Sometimes you make the right decision, sometimes you make the decision right."

H. L. Hunt
- "Decide what you want, decide what you are willing to exchange for it. Establish your priorities and go to work."

Henri-Frederic Amiel
- "The man who insists upon seeing with perfect clearness before he decides, never decides."

MAKE DECISIVE DECISIONS

Jim Rohn
- "It doesn't matter which side of the fence you get off on sometimes. What matters most is getting off. You cannot make progress without making decisions."

- "Indecision is the thief of opportunity."

Learned Hand
- "Life is made up of a series of judgments on insufficient data, and if we waited to run down all our doubts, it would flow past us."

Oprah Winfrey
- "One of the biggest lessons I've learned recently is that when you don't know what to do, you should do nothing until you figure out what to do because a lot of times you feel like you are pressed against the wall, and you've got to make a decision. You never have to do anything. Don't know what to do? Do nothing."

Peter Drucker
- "Making good decisions is a crucial skill at every level."

T. Boone Pickens
- "Be willing to make decisions. That's the most important quality in a good leader. Don't fall victim to what I call the ready-aim-aim-aim-aim syndrome. You must be willing to fire."

Tony Robbins
- "More than anything else, I believe it's our decisions, not the conditions of our lives, that determine our destiny."

- "A real decision is measured by the fact that you've taken new action. If there's no action, you haven't truly decided."

- "Stay committed to your decisions, but stay flexible in your approach."

41

Problems Present Opportunities For You To Learn And Grow

Jerry's Tips:

- Problems are part of life. Accept that fact and you will instantly become more confident and less worried about your future.

- Don't put off solving a problem. Problems are like weeds, they grow if ignored.

- When you have a problem don't focus on 'why' something cannot be done, think 'how' you can do it.

- There is a solution to every problem.

- Your greatest learning and improvement comes from trying to solve your problems.

- Successful people enjoy solving problems.

- Ask lots of questions to solve problems.

- Make sure you clearly know what the problem is before you move on to thinking about ways to solve it by getting into the habit to always ask this crucial question when you start to consider a problem: 'what is the problem you are trying to solve?'

- Each time you confront a problem and think through its solution you learn a lot and become better skilled at solving problems.

- Solving problems is like exercising with weights to build strength or running to improve your endurance. The more problems you solve the stronger you become to confront and focus on any problem to solve it.

PROBLEMS PRESENT OPPORTUNITIES FOR YOU TO LEARN AND GROW

Aristotle Onassis
- "We must free ourselves of the hope that the sea will ever rest. We must learn to sail in high winds."

Charles F. Kettering
- "A problem well stated is a problem half solved."

Denis Waitley
- "Don't dwell on what went wrong. Instead, focus on what to do next. Spend your energies on moving forward toward finding the answer."

Donald Trump
- "When confronted with a problem I always ask myself, 'Is this a blip, or a catastrophe?' – it gives me a point of reason in the midst of bad news. Your problems can be temporary if you keep your momentum moving forward. We all experience difficulties, but they can be blips if you remain positive and move on."

Henry Ford
- "Don't find fault. Find a remedy."

- "Most people spend more time and energy going around problems than in trying to solve them."

Lao Tzu
- "Face the simple fact before it comes involved. Solve the small problem before it becomes big."

- "The biggest problem in the world could have been solved when it was small."

Mike Leavitt
- "There is a time in the life of every problem when it is big enough to see, yet small enough to solve."

Norman Vincent Peale
- "The only people that don't have problems are in a cemetery."

- "Problems are to the mind what exercise is to the muscles, they toughen and make strong."

THE SUCCESS FORMULA FOR PERSONAL GROWTH

- "Your whole life can change by solving a problem."

- "God gives us problems to push back against to sculpt our souls."

- "How you think about a problem is more important than the problem itself - so always think positively."

- "Believe it is possible to solve your problem. Tremendous things happen to the believer. So believe the answer will come. It will."

- "Problems are a sign of life."

- "Problems are a gift."

Rene Descartes
- "Each problem that I solved became a rule which served afterwards to solve other problems."

Robert Kiyosaki
- "Inside of every problem lies an opportunity."

Theodore Isaac Rubin
- "The problem is not that there are problems. The problem is expecting otherwise and thinking that having problems is a problem."

Tony Robbins
- "Your problems are gifts. They give you choices to learn and grow by solving them."

- "We must learn to view our problems as something good not bad."

- "Sometimes the biggest mistake we make is in thinking that we should have no problems. We think problems are a curse, instead of knowing that our problems are a gift. The only way we usually grow is if we get a good enough problem to stimulate us to use our resourcefulness to find a part of our self that is not being used."

Voltaire
- "There is no problem that can withstand the assault of sustained thinking."

42

Learn From Your Setbacks And Mistakes

Jerry's Tips:

- Failing at something is an 'event,' it does not mean 'you' are a failure.

- The successful person's mindset is, that when they encounter a setback or make a mistake they view the situation as an opportunity for them to learn from the situation and improve themselves, so they will be prepared to do better next time.

- There is no such thing as failure; only results. If your results are not good, learn from them and change what you're doing to get better results.

- When you have a setback or make a mistake, honestly ask yourself: 'Is there anything I could have done differently to avoid this situation?' and apply that knowledge going forward.

- It is very good for you to use self-criticism to identify what you may have done wrong following a setback, mistake or failure so you learn from the experience. It helps you grow! But don't confuse self-criticism with putting yourself down for the situation.

- When you learn from setbacks, mistakes and failure you learn what not to do again.

- It's ok to try something and fail. But you must analyze and learn from the failure so you won't repeat it next time.

- You must work to learn from each failure what not to do to avoid repeating the mistake.

- You need to scrutinize your failures with a laser beam to honestly figure out why you did not succeed so you can learn and improve and not make the same mistake, or have the same outcome next time.

THE SUCCESS FORMULA FOR PERSONAL GROWTH

- Successful people bounce back from failure, setbacks, opposition, hardship, defeat, discouragement and personal misfortune.

- Failure is a quitter's word – don't refer to what you've ever done as a failure. Instead use the word setback or mistake to remind yourself you can overcome it.

- We can only learn to walk and run by falling down a lot.

- Enjoy falling down. It means you are learning something new.

- "To succeed you must fail so that you'll know what doesn't work and what not to do the next time."

- Don't view your failures, setbacks or mistakes as permanent. They present opportunities to learn and have greater success.

- Many famous people failed over and over before they succeeded. This proves you can succeed no matter how many times you fail if you don't quit and keep improving.

Abraham Maslow
- "It seems that the necessary thing to do is not to fear mistakes, to plunge in, to do the best that one can, hoping to learn enough from blunders to correct them eventually."

Albert Einstein
- "Anyone who has never made a mistake has never tried anything new."

Barack Obama
- "Making your mark on the world is hard. If it were easy, everybody would do it. But it's not. It takes patience, it takes commitment, and it comes with plenty of failure along the way. The real test is not whether you avoid this failure, because you won't. It's whether you let it harden or shame you into inaction, or whether you learn from it; whether you choose to persevere."

Benjamin Disraeli
- "There is no education like adversity."

LEARN FROM YOUR SETBACKS AND MISTAKES

Benjamin Fairless
- "When things go wrong. Just do two things:
  1. Ask yourself, 'What can I do to make myself more deserving of the next opportunity?'
  2. Don't waste time and energy being discouraged. Don't berate yourself. Plan to win next time."

Bernice Johnson Reagon
- "Life's challenges are not supposed to paralyze you, they're supposed to help you discover who you are."

Bill Gates
- "It's fine to celebrate success but it is more important to heed the lessons of failure."

Confucius
- "Our greatest glory is not in never falling, but in rising every time we fall."

Dale Carnegie
- "When fate hands you a lemon, make lemonade."

- "The successful man will profit from his mistakes and try again in a different way."

David J. Schwartz
- "How you think when you lose determines how long it will be until you win."

Donald Trump
- "What separates the winners from the losers is how a person reacts to each new twist of fate."

- "I'm a firm believer in learning from adversity. Often the worst of times can turn to your advantage - my life is a study of that."

Dr. Maxwell Maltz
- "The path to success is never a straight line. It zig zags with ups and downs and failures, disappointments until you reach your goals and success."

THE SUCCESS FORMULA FOR PERSONAL GROWTH

Henry Ford
- "Failure is simply the opportunity to begin again, this time more intelligently."

- "Even a mistake may turn out to be the one thing necessary to a worthwhile achievement."

Horace
- "Adversity has the effect of eliciting talents, which in prosperous circumstances would have lain dormant."

Jack Welch
- "I've learned that mistakes can often be as good a teacher as success."

Joan Collins
- "Show me a person who has never made a mistake and I'll show you somebody who has never achieved much."

John Keats
- "Failure is in a sense the highway to success, as each discovery of what is false leads us to seek earnestly after what is true."

John McEnroe
- "The important thing is to learn a lesson every time you lose. Life is a learning process and you have to try to learn what's best for you."

John Sculley
- "I have found that I always learn more from my mistakes than from my successes. If you aren't making some mistakes, you aren't taking enough chances."

Lao Tzu
- "Failure is the foundation of success, and the means by which it is achieved."

Les Brown
- "If you view all the things that happen to you, both good and bad, as opportunities, then you operate out of a higher level of consciousness."

Malcolm S. Forbes
- "Failure is success if we learn from it."

LEARN FROM YOUR SETBACKS AND MISTAKES

Michael Jordan
- "I have missed more than 9,000 shots in my career. I have lost almost 300 games. On 26 occasions I have been entrusted to take the game winning shot . . . and missed. And I have failed over and over and over again in my life. And that is why . . . I succeed."

- "Always turn a negative situation into a positive situation."

Morihei Ueshiba
- "Failure is the key to success; each mistake teaches us something."

Og Mandino
- "Each struggle, each defeat sharpens your skills and strengthens your courage and your endurance."

Oprah Winfrey
- "Do the one thing you think you cannot do. Fail at it. Try again. Do better the second time. The only people who never tumble are those who never mount the high wire. This is your moment. Own it."

Paul (Bear) Bryant
- "When you make a mistake, there are only three things you should ever do about it: admit it, learn from it, and don't repeat it."

Peter McWilliams
- "Mistakes, obviously, show us what needs improving. Without mistakes, how would we know what we had to work on?"

Napoleon Bonaparte
- "You become strong by defying defeat and by turning loss into gain and failure to success."

Napoleon Hill
- "Every adversity, every failure, and every headache carries with it the seed for an equivalent or greater benefit."

- "Most great people have attained their greatest success just one step beyond their greatest failure."

Roger Von Oech
- "Remember the two benefits of failure. First, if you do fail, you learn what doesn't work; and second, the failure gives you the opportunity to try a new approach."

Samuel Smiles

- "It is a mistake to suppose that men succeed through success; they much oftener succeed through failures. Precept, study, advice, and example could never have taught them so well as failure has done."

- "We learn wisdom from failure much more than from success. We often discover what will do, by finding out what will not do; and probably he who never made a mistake never made a discovery."

Soichiro Honda

- "Success is 99% failure."

Sophocles

- "There is no sense in crying over spilt milk. Why bewail what is done and cannot be recalled?"

Steve Jobs

- "Sometimes when you innovate, you make mistakes. It is best to admit them quickly and get on with improving your other innovations."

Steven Covey

- "When you make a mistake, admit it, correct it, and learn from it - immediately."

Thomas Edison

- "I have not failed. I've just found 10,000 ways that won't work."

- "I am not discouraged, because every wrong attempt discarded is another step forward."

Tony Robbins

- "When you temporarily run aground, remember that there are no failures in life. There are only results. Consider the adage: Success is the result of good judgment, good judgment is the result of experience, and experience is often the result of bad judgment!"

- "You must learn how to handle frustration.
Look at almost any great success, and you'll find there has been massive frustration along the way. If you learn how to handle more frustration you will be able to achieve more.

A simple two-step formula:

LEARN FROM YOUR SETBACKS AND MISTAKES

1. Don't sweat the small stuff, and
2. Remember, it's all small stuff."

W. Clement Stone
- "With every disadvantage there is always a greater advantage."

- "Every great man, every successful man, no matter what the field of endeavor, has known the magic that lies in these words: every adversity has the seed of an equivalent or greater benefit."

- "Like success, failure is many things to many people. With Positive Mental Attitude, failure is a learning experience, a rung on the ladder, a plateau at which to get your thoughts in order and prepare to try again."

Winston Churchill
- "Success is going from failure to failure without a loss of enthusiasm."

Zig Ziglar
- "If you learn from defeat, you haven't really lost."

- "Failure is a detour, not a dead-end street."

- "Sometimes adversity is what you need to face in order to become successful."

- "Failure is an event, not a person."

- "It's not what happens to you that determines how far you will go in life; it is how you handle what happens to you."

43

Always Do The Right Thing

Jerry's Tips:

- Don't just do things right, do the right things.

- If you know it's not right, don't do it.

Brian Tracy
- "Refuse to compromise what you know to be right for anyone or anything."

- "Disciplining yourself to do what you know is right and important, although difficult, is the high road to pride, self esteem, and personal satisfaction."

General Norman Schwarzkopf
- "Do what is right, not what you think the high headquarters wants or what you think will make you look good."

John Wooden
- "If you don't have time to do it right, when will you have time to do it over?"

Kareem Abdul Jabbar
- "I try to do the right thing at the right time. They may just be little things, but usually they make the difference between winning and losing."

Martin Luther King, Jr.
- "The time is always right to do what is right."

Peter Drucker
- "Start with what is right rather than what is acceptable."

Always Do the Right Thing

W. Clement Stone

"Have the courage to say no. Have the courage to face the truth. Do the right thing because it is right. These are the magic keys to living your life with integrity."

44

Change Before You Have To, The World And Your Life Do Not Stand Still

Jerry's Tips:

- The most successful people and organizations recognize change quickly, embrace and adapt to the changes, and implement it into their daily routine.

- Nothing stands still. Even if you are currently successful you must change to remain successful.

- Keep a sharp eye peeled to see change coming before it arrives.

Adlai E. Stevenson
- "Change is inevitable. Change for the better is a full-time job."

Anonymous
- "The bend in the road is not the end of the road unless you refuse to take the turn."

Brian Tracy
- "Resolve to be a master of change rather than a victim of change."

Bruce Lee
- "Man, he is constantly growing and when he is bound by a set pattern of ideas or way of doing things, that's when he stops growing."

Catherine Pulsifer
- "If you resist change, you will face challenges on a daily basis. If you consciously refocus your attitude to see the benefits of change, your outlook becomes positive and life becomes easier."

CHANGE BEFORE YOU HAVE TO, THE WORLD AND YOUR LIFE DO NOT STAND STILL

Charles Darwin
- "It is not the strongest of the species who survive, not the most intelligent, but those who are the most adaptive to change."

Dr. Spencer Johnston
- "If you do not change, you can become extinct. Get out of your comfort zone and adapt to change sooner. Take control, rather than let things happen to you."

Eric Hoffer
- "In times of change, learners inherit the Earth, while the learned find themselves beautifully equipped to deal with a world that no longer exists."

George Bernard Shaw
- "Progress is impossible without change; and those who cannot change their minds, cannot change anything."

Heraclitus
- "Nothing is permanent but change."

Isaac Asimov
- "It is change, continuing change, inevitable change, that is the dominant factor in society today. No sensible decision can be made any longer without taking into account not only the world as it is, but the world as it will be."

Jack Welch
- "Change before you have to."

John F. Kennedy
- "Change is the law of life. And those who look only to the past or present are certain to miss future."

Lee Iacocca
- "The most successful businessman is the man who holds onto the old just as long as it is good, and grabs the new just as soon as it is better."

THE SUCCESS FORMULA FOR PERSONAL GROWTH

Leonardo da Vinci
- "Life is pretty simple: You do some stuff. Most fails. Some works. You do more of what works. If it works big, others quickly copy it. Then you do something else. The trick is the doing something else."

Maya Angelou
- "If you don't like something, change it. If you can't change it, change your attitude. Don't complain."

Nido Qubein
- "Change brings opportunity."

Nolan Ryan
- "Enjoying success requires the ability to adapt. Only by being open to change will you have a true opportunity to get the most from your talent."

Peter Drucker
- "The entrepreneur always searches for change, responds to it, and exploits it as an opportunity."

Phil Jackson
- "The most consistent thing about life is that nothing is the same, everything changes. If you can accept that, then you're OK. If you can't accept the fact that you can't control everything, then you get yourself in a rut."

Steven Hawking
- "Intelligence is the ability to adapt to change."

Wayne Gretzky
- "I skate to where the puck will be."

Zig Ziglar
- "Little men with little minds and little imaginations go through life in little ruts, smuggling resisting all changes that would jar their little worlds."

45

Destroy Your Limiting Beliefs And Toxic Self-Talk To Stop Holding Yourself Back

Jerry's Tips:

- Limiting beliefs such as 'I can't be rich,' or 'I can't have a happy marriage' hold you back and set a ceiling of what is possible or not possible for you.

- Listen to your inner thoughts. Are you leading yourself to happiness and success or to unhappiness and failure?

- Conquer you limiting beliefs and nothing can prevent you from achieving success in anything you want.

- Examine your negative thoughts for false assumptions or beliefs, and change them.

- Think of why you are not successful. It's so easy to come up with a long list. Now think of how you can become successful – How come you now have very few or no ideas? The answer is you have been conditioned to think you cannot be successful. But successful people don't think like that. They can come up with a list of ways to be a success because they are conditioned and taught by their parents, teachers and friends that they can, and more importantly, will be, very successful.

- We're afraid we can't be successful and we're afraid we can.

    If we know what we want to accomplish in life but we belief we can't have it, we're left to deal with all the feelings of undeservability, disappointment and limitation with which we surround ourselves.

    If we decide we can have it, we're forced to face up to actually doing what it would take to make it happen.

THE SUCCESS FORMULA FOR PERSONAL GROWTH

Rather than deal with these two hard choices we subconsciously make a third choice - we pretend not to know what we want out of life. Or, even better, we decide not to want anything at all.

- Break through your fear of knowing what you really want to do in your life.

- It's hard for people to consider what their purpose is in life and what they want out of life.

- Instead of focusing on why something cannot be done think how you can do it.

- If you have an attitude of 'Okay, I'll give it a try, but I don't think it will work' you have failed before you start.

- Become aware of your self talk; what is that voice inside your head saying to you all day?

- Your negative self-talk is like a virus that infects your self-esteem and self-confidence.

- Don't listen to the voice of negativity. Listen to your voice of possibility!

- Be your own best friend, not your own worst enemy.

- Build yourself up, don't put yourself down.

- Transform your negative self-talk into positive praise.

- Don't psych yourself out, psych yourself up!

Andy and Larry Wachowski
   [Morpheus to Neo in the Movie 'The Matrix'
      the scene where Morpheus is training Neo Karate]

DESTROY YOUR LIMITING BELIEFS AND TOXIC SELF-TALK TO STOP HOLDING YOURSELF BACK

- "What are you waiting for? You're faster than this. Don't 'think' you are, know you are. Come on. Stop 'trying' to hit me and 'hit' me."

Anonymous
- "Never believe your doubts and never doubt your beliefs."

David J. Schwartz
- "The number one obstacle on the road to high-level success is the feeling that major accomplishment is beyond reach. This attitude stems from many, many suppressive forces that direct our thinking toward mediocre levels."

Denis Waitley
- "Relentless, repetitive self talk is what changes our self-image."

- "The most important key to the permanent enhancement of self esteem is the practice of positive inner-talk."

Elbert Hubbard
- "The greatest mistake you can make in life is to be continually fearing you will make one."

Franklin D. Roosevelt
- "Men are not prisoners of fate, but only prisoners of their own minds."

George Lucas
  [Master Yoda to Luke Skywalker in the Movie 'Star Wars']
- "Do, or Do Not. There is no Try."

- "Our life is what our thoughts make it. A man will find that as he alters his thoughts toward things and other people, things and other people will alter towards him."

Jack Nicklaus
- "Sometimes the biggest problem is in your head. You've got to believe you can play a shot instead of wondering where your next bad shot is coming from."

Lao Tzu
- "When you correct your mind, everything else falls into place."

Les Brown
- "People think too much about what they 'think' their limitations are instead of thinking they can do things and accomplish them."

Marcus Aurelius
- "If you are distressed by anything external, the pain is not due to the thing itself but to your own estimate of it; and this you have the power to revoke at any moment."

Mark Twain
- "It ain't what you don't know that gets you into trouble. It's what you know for sure that just ain't so."

Norman Vincent Peale
- "Change your thoughts and you change your world."

Oprah Winfrey
- "The greatest discovery of all time is that a person can change his future by merely changing his attitude."

Pat Croce
- "Some of you might be thinking that your setbacks are too steep. That the obstacles and problems and competitive challenges in the marketplace are too numerous to overcome. That the competitors are too strong to conquer. That your dreams and deadlines are impossible.

  NO NO NO!! Just like your moms have told you and your grand moms have told you - tell your kids, the only place where it's impossible rests on top of your shoulders.

  UNLOCK YOUR MINDS. YOU HAVE THE KEYS!!"

Steven Covey
- "We are limited but we can push back the borders of our limitations."

Terry Cole-Whittaker
- "What you think of me is none of my business."

Tony Robbins
- "The only thing that's keeping you from getting what you want is the story you keep telling yourself."

Destroy Your Limiting Beliefs and Toxic Self-Talk to Stop Holding Yourself Back

- "Nothing has any power over me other than that which I give it through my conscious thoughts."

- "Take control of your consistent emotions and begin to consciously and deliberately reshape your daily experience of life."

- "All personal breakthroughs begin with a change in beliefs. So how do we change? The most effective way is to get your brain to associate massive pain to the old belief. You must feel deep in your gut that not only has this belief cost you pain in the past, but it's costing you in the present and, ultimately, can only bring you pain in the future. Then you must associate tremendous pleasure to the idea of adopting a new, empowering belief."

- "The truth is that we can learn to condition our minds, bodies, and emotions to link pain or pleasure to whatever we choose. By changing what we link pain and pleasure to, we will instantly change our behaviors."

- "What we can or cannot do, what we consider possible or impossible, is rarely a function of our true capability. It is more likely a function of our beliefs about who we are."

- "The secret of success is learning how to use pain and pleasure instead of having pain and pleasure use you. If you do that, you're in control of your life. If you don't, life controls you."

- "We will act consistently with our view of who we truly are, whether that view is accurate or not."

- "Nothing in life has any real meaning except the meaning you give it."

Vince Lombardi
- "We would accomplish many more things if we did not think of them as impossible."

Wayne Dyer
- "When you change the way you look at things, the things you look at change."

Willie Nelson
- "Once you replace negative thoughts with positive ones, you'll start having positive results."

Zig Ziglar
- "You are what you are and where you are because of what has gone into your mind. You can change what you are and where you are by changing what goes into your mind."

46

Conquer Your Fear

Jerry's Tips:

- If you are afraid to do something, prepare to do it, and then do it – your fear will be gone and you will feel great!

- You build confidence and courage each time you do what you fear to do.

- Conquer fear and worry by doing what you fear and worry about.

- Don't waste time thinking and being afraid of your fear. Instead, spend your time taking action to overcome your fear.

- When you are fearful, immediately snap yourself out of it by thinking positive thoughts and taking action to conquer your fear.

- Anxiety before a big event is normal. It prepares you to do your best.

- Fear of failure and fear of rejection only have power if you give it to them.

- To overcome your fears, develop a mindset that you can accomplish anything, and that you always learn and become stronger from experiences that challenge you.

Aristotle
- "You will never do anything in this world without courage. It is the greatest quality of the mind next to honor."

Babe Ruth
- "Don't let the fear of striking out hold you back."

Bill Cosby
- "Decide that you want it more than you are afraid of it."

- "In order to succeed, your desire for success should be greater than your fear of failure."

Chuck Norris
- "Running from your fear can be more painful than facing it, for better or worse."

Chin-Ning Chu
- "In spite of fear, do what you have to do."

Dale Carnegie
- "You can conquer almost any fear if you will only make up your mind to do so. For remember, fear doesn't exist anywhere except in the mind."

- "Do the thing you fear to do and keep on doing it... that is the quickest and surest way ever yet discovered to conquer fear."

- "Inaction breeds doubt and fear. Action breeds confidence and courage. If you want to conquer fear, do not sit home and think about it. Go out and get busy."

- "If you can't sleep, then get up and do something instead of lying there worrying. It's the worry that gets you, not the lack of sleep."

- "Instead of worrying about what people say of you, why not spend time trying to accomplish something they will admire."

- "You can conquer almost any fear if you will only make up your mind to do so. For remember, fear doesn't exist anywhere except in the mind."

David J. Schwartz
- "Do what you fear and fear disappears."

- "Hesitation only enlarges, magnifies the fear. Take action promptly. Be decisive."

- "Action cures fear."

CONQUER YOUR FEAR

- "Put the actions principle to work. Next time you experience big fear or little fear; steady yourself. Then search for an answer to this question: What kind of action can I take to conquer my fear?"

- "Isolate your fear. Then take appropriate action."

- "Use action to cure fear and gain confidence."

- "Action feeds and strengthens confidence; inaction in all forms feeds fear. To fight fear, act. To increase fear – wait, put off, postpone."

- "In brief, it really is easy to forget the unpleasant if we simply refuse to recall it. Withdraw only positive thoughts from your memory bank. Let the others fade away. And your confidence, that feeling of being on top of the world, will zoom up-ward. You take a big step forward toward conquering your fear when you refuse to remember negative, self-deprecating thoughts."

Donald Trump
- "Do not allow fear to settle into place in any part of your life. It is a defeating attitude and a negative emotion. Recognize and zap it immediately. Replace it with a problem - solving attitude, faith in yourself, and hard work. Put that formula into working order for yourself and you'll be dealing from a position of power, not fear. That's winning."

Earl Nightingale
- "Whenever we're afraid, it's because we don't know enough. If we understood enough, we would never be afraid."

Eleanor Roosevelt
- "I believe that anyone can conquer fear by doing the things he fears to do."

- "You gain strength, courage and confidence by every experience in which you really stop to look fear in the face. You are able to say to yourself, 'I have lived through this horror. I can take the next thing that comes along.' You must do the thing you think you cannot do."

Frank Herbert
- "I must not fear. Fear is the mind-killer. Fear is the little-death that brings total obliteration. I will face my fear. I will permit it to pass over me and through me. And when it has gone past I will turn the inner eye to see its path. Where the fear has gone there will be nothing. Only I will remain."

General George S. Patton
- "Do not fear failure."

Henry Ford
- "One of the greatest discoveries a man makes, one of his great surprises, is to find he can do what he was afraid he couldn't do."

James Allen
- "They who have conquered doubt and fear have conquered failure."

Jeff Keller
- "Do the thing you fear and the fear will dissipate."

- "Successful people have fears but they take action and move forward despite them."

Jiddu Krishnamurti
- "Do you know your particular fears? And what do you usually do with them? You run away from them, don't you, or invent ideas and images to cover them? But to run away from fear is only to increase it."

John Wayne
- "Courage is being scared to death -- and saddling up anyway."

Les Brown
- "When you face your fear, most of the time you will discover that it was not really such a big threat after all. We all need some form of deeply rooted, powerful motivation – it empowers us to overcome obstacles so we can live our dreams."

- "When you step into your fears and continue to push yourself to go on something happens for you – it will enable you to transcend yourself."

Marie Curie
- "Nothing in life is to be feared. It is only to be understood."

Dr. Maxwell Maltz
- "Everyday living requires courage if life is to be effective and bring happiness."

Napoleon Hill
- "Fear is nothing but faith in reverse gear! The foundation on which both faith and fear rests is belief in something."

Norman Vincent Peale
- "Action is a great restorer and builder of confidence. Inaction is not only the result, but the cause, of fear. Perhaps the action you take will be successful; perhaps different action or adjustments will have to follow. But any action is better than no action at all."

Og Mandino
- "To conquer fear I must always act without hesitation and the flutters in my heart will vanish."

Oprah Winfrey
- "The thing you fear most has no power. Your fear of it is what has the power. Facing the truth really will set you free."

Ralph Waldo Emerson
- "Do the thing you fear and the death of fear is certain."

- "Fear defeats more people than any other one thing in the world."

- "Always do what you are afraid to do."

- "A hero is no braver than an ordinary man, but he is braver five minutes longer."

Rosa Parks
- "I have learned over the years that when one's mind is made up, this diminishes fear; knowing what must be done does away with fear."

Sven Goran Eriksson
- "The greatest barrier to success is the fear of failure."

Theodore Roosevelt
- "I have often been afraid, but I would not give in to it. I made myself act as though I was not afraid and gradually my fear disappeared."

Tony Robbins
- "Let fear be a counselor and not a jailer."

W. Clement Stone
- "Thinking will not overcome fear but action will."

47

Reject Rejection!

Jerry's Tips:

- If someone rejects you, instead of thinking they don't like you, say to yourself: 'How can I change my approach to get what I want?'

- Rejection can only impact your self-worth if 'you' let it.

- Never take rejection personally.

- Learn and improve from any rejection.

- Rejection does not bother a majestic mountain or an ocean. You should be friendly on the outside and like a mountain and ocean in the inside. This means that your ability to love yourself and respect yourself should not come from whether other people approve or disapprove of you.

Ashley Tisdale
- "Don't let anyone, or any rejection, keep you from what you want."

Bo Bennett
- "It is not rejection itself that people fear, it is the possible consequences of rejection. Preparing to accept those consequences and viewing rejection as a learning experience that will bring you closer to success, will not only help you to conquer the fear of rejection, but help you to appreciate rejection itself."

- "A rejection is nothing more than a necessary step in the pursuit of success."

Marcus Aurelius
- "Reject your sense of injury and the injury itself disappears."

Sylvester Stallone
- "I take rejection as someone blowing a bugle in my ear to wake me up and get going, rather than retreat."

Tony Robbins
- "You must learn how to handle rejection. To succeed, you must learn how to cope with a little word 'no', learn how to strip that rejection of all its power. The best salesmen are those who are rejected most. They are the ones who can take any 'no' and use it as a prod to go onto the next 'yes'."

48

Eliminate Your Unsuccessful Thoughts And Actions

Jerry's Tips:

- Stop doing things that don't get you where you want to go!

- For everything you may do in life you must get into the habit to ask yourself: 'Will this get me closer to my goals?' If not, don't do it or do it only for a brief time to give you some relaxation.

- No car race has ever been won by a team that puts the wrong gas in the tank and then has to take time to refill it with the right gas. To win, you must eliminate everything that does not put you closer to achieving your goals.

Anonymous
- "Old habits die hard."

Bruce Lee
- "It's not the daily increase but daily decrease. Hack away at the unessential."

Benjamin Franklin
- "A small leak can sink a great ship."

- "Each year one vicious habit discarded, in time might make the worst of us good."

THE SUCCESS FORMULA FOR PERSONAL GROWTH

David J. Schwartz
- "Eliminate the word impossible from your thinking and speaking vocabularies. Impossible is a failure word. The thought 'It's impossible' sets off a chain reaction of other thoughts to prove you're right."

Ed Parker
- "A man should be like a sculptor who gets a piece of granite and chips away the unessentials to get the true image of his imagination."

Jim Rohn
- "Nourish the mind like you would your body. The mind cannot survive on junk food."

Michelangelo
- "Every block of stone has a statue inside it and it is the task of the sculptor to discover it."

Miyamoto Musashi
- "Do nothing which is of no use."

49

Learn To Turn Off Stress And Perform Well Under Pressure

Jerry's Tips:

- If you adopt the mindset all day long that you look forward to challenging yourself and growing from the experience, you will no longer feel pressure; you will simply do your best in any situation and enjoy it.

- Pressure is created by how we look at a particular situation or encounter with a person. It is not the situation or the other person that makes us tense, it is us! We create pressure by imagining a negative outcome. The solution is to train your mind to always perform naturally without thinking about what it needs to do next and what the possible consequences are of your actions. Be in the moment.

- The objective under pressure, is not to be able to perform superbly, because that is an unreasonable goal; your objective in very important situations should be to perform the same way you would if you didn't think a lot was on the line.

- If you think about failing you probably will fail. So don't think about it. Instead, think about how good you will feel after you accomplish what you are trying to do.

Michael Jordan
- "I never looked at the consequences of missing a big shot... when you think about the consequences you always think of a negative result."

Sebastian Coe
- "All pressure is self-inflicted. It's what you make of it or how you let it rub off on you."

Wayne Dyer

"Next time you're stressed, ask yourself, what would my ideal self do right now? And then act as if you were that ideal self. You don't need to do that for too long until you are that ideal."

50

Get Comfortable Being Uncomfortable, Go Outside Your "Comfort Zone" To Improve

Jerry's Tips:

- Go outside your Comfort Zone to bring more success inside your life.

- If you are too comfortable in life you are not growing as an individual.

- All activity that develops and improves you is uncomfortable because it is something you are not used to.

- Lifting weights for exercise is uncomfortable but it makes you strong – This is a great life lesson.

- Appreciate doing things that make you feel uncomfortable because it's a sign you are developing.

- When a mother gives birth she is very uncomfortable, but through that painful experience she brings forth the greatest accomplishment – the birth of a human being. It's the same with your life. If you step outside your Comfort Zone you will give birth to great new abilities in yourself!

Andre Gide
- "You cannot discover new oceans unless you have the courage to lose sight of the shore."

THE SUCCESS FORMULA FOR PERSONAL GROWTH

Anonymous
"I used to have a comfort zone where I knew I wouldn't fail.
The same four walls and busywork were really more like jail.
I longed so much to do the things I'd never done before,
But stayed inside my comfort zone and paced the same old floor.
I said it didn't matter that I wasn't doing much.
I said I didn't care for things like commission checks and such.
I claimed to be so busy with the things inside the zone,
But deep inside I longed for something special of my own.

I couldn't let my life go by just watching others win.
I held my breath; I stepped outside and let the change begin.
I took a step and with new strength I'd never felt before,

I kissed my comfort zone goodbye and closed and locked the door.
If you're in a comfort zone, afraid to venture out,
Remember that all winners were at one time filled with doubt.
A step or two and words of praise can make your dreams come true.
Reach for your future with a smile; success is there for you!"

Brian Tracy
"Move out of your comfort zone. You can only grow if you are willing to feel awkward and uncomfortable when you try something new."

Catherine Pulsifer
"If you remain in your comfort zone you will not go any further."

Pablo Picasso
"I am always doing that which I cannot do, in order that I may learn how to do it."

Ralph Waldo Emerson
"Do not be too timid and squeamish about your actions. All life is an experiment. The more experiments you make the better. What if they are a little course and you may get your coat soiled or torn? What if you do fail, and get fairly rolled in the dirt once or twice. Up again, you shall never be so afraid of a tumble."

GET COMFORTABLE BEING UNCOMFORTABLE, GO OUTSIDE YOUR "COMFORT ZONE" TO IMPROVE

Seth Godin
- "My new favorite word is 'awkward.'...The reason we need to be in search of awkward is that awkward is the barrier between us and excellence, between where we are and the remarkable. If it were easy, everyone would have done it already, and it wouldn't be worth the effort."

51

Meditate

To Reduce Stress, Calm Your Mind, Improve Your Focus And Concentration

Jerry's Tips:

- Meditation allows you to recharge your motivational batteries. When you are feeling down or depressed take a break and recharge yourself by meditating for a while to calm your busy mind, center yourself and energize yourself.

- It is not enough to only be able to reach a state of complete relaxation by meditating at the top of a mountain, or being the wise man in a cave where the surroundings are calm. You need to be able to have a calm mind when the surroundings are stormy and throughout your daily life.

- Meditation develops in you the power to remain calm, centered and focused, and to perform at your peak level of performance.

Blaise Pascal
- "All men's miseries derive from not being able to sit in a quiet room alone."

George Bernard Shaw
- "Imagination is the beginning of creation. You imagine what you desire, you will what you imagine and at last you create what you will."

Mark Victor Hansen
- "In imagination, there's no limitation."

MEDITATE TO REDUCE STRESS, CALM YOUR MIND, IMPROVE YOUR FOCUS AND CONCENTRATION

Michael Phelps
- "You can't put a limit on anything. The more you dream, the farther you get."

Napoleon Hill
- "Hold a picture of yourself long and steadily enough in your mind's eye, and you will be drawn toward it."

Norman Vincent Peale
- "If you paint in your mind a picture of bright and happy expectations, you put yourself into a condition conducive to your goal."

Pythagoras
- "Learn to be silent. Let your quiet mind listen and absorb."

52

Use Visualizations

To Train Your Mind
To Accomplish Anything

Jerry's Tips:

- We can become what we imagine.

- Visualization is mental rehearsal for whatever you want to do or accomplish in life.

- When you visualize and imagine something in your mind with sufficient emotional content and vivid detail you plant the seeds in your mind that will grow into the reality you desire.

- The greatest successes in business, sports, and other human activities, that reward successs, all involved people who deeply imagined their success in their mind and then brought it to life.

Albert Einstein
- "Imagination is everything. It is the preview of life's coming attractions."

- "Imagination is more important than knowledge. Knowledge is limited. Imagination encircles the world."

Belva Davis
- "Don't be afraid of the space between your dreams and reality. If you can dream it, you can make it so."

Use Visualizations to Train Your Mind to Accomplish Anything

Bob Boshnack

- "The power of the mind and visual imagery can be further understood by simply thinking how when we are hungry and think about our favorite food, our mouths begin to water; or when we hear fantastic news, a rush of good feelings envelops us; or when we hear horrible news, we feel a gut ripping sensation in the pit of our stomachs.
Remember that every great work and discovery first existed in someone's mind as a vivid image. Every act and deed that has enabled man to excel and achieve success was first born in someone's mind.

  Make no doubt about it, intense positive thinking and visual imagery can change your life. The ability to translate one's hope and aspirations into positive sensory-rich images is the cutting edge which separates the high achiever from the run-of-the-mill everyday person.

  THE SUSTAINED INTENSITY OF YOUR POSITIVE THOUGHTS AND DETAILED MENTAL VISUALIZATION WILL CREATE A POWERFUL ATTRACTION FORCE DRAWING YOU TO WHAT YOU VISUALIZE AND THINK ABOUT MOST. YOU CAN BE YOUR OWN FORTUNE TELLER BY VISUALIZING, CONTROLLING, AND DIRECTING INTO POSITIVE ACTION, THE THOUGHTS AND CONCERNS OF YOUR MIND!"

David J. Schwartz

- "Look at things not as they are, but as they can be. Visualization adds value to everything."

- "A big thinker always visualizes what can be done in the future. He isn't stuck with the present."

Charles A. Garfield

- "I've discovered that numerous peak performers use the skill of mental rehearsal of visualization. They mentally run through important events before they happen."

- "Peak performers develop powerful mental images of the behavior that will lead to the desired results. They see in their mind's eye the result they want, and the actions leading to it."

THE SUCCESS FORMULA FOR PERSONAL GROWTH

Earl Nightingale

- "Picture yourself in your minds eye as having already achieved this goal. See yourself doing the things you'll be doing when you've reached your goal."

- "Whatever we plant in our subconscious mind and nourish with repetition and emotion will one day become a reality."

Dr. Maxwell Maltz

- "When you see a thing clearly in your mind, your creative 'success mechanism' within you takes over and does the job much better than you could do it by conscious effort or 'willpower.'"

Robert Collier

- "Our subconscious minds have no sense of humor, play no jokes and cannot tell the difference between reality and an imagined thought or image. What we continually think about eventually will manifest in our lives."

- "Any thought that is passed on to the subconscious often enough and convincingly enough is finally accepted."

- "Visualize this thing that you want, see it, feel it, believe in it. Make your mental blue print, and begin to build."

Ruben Gonzalez

- "The mind can't tell the difference between something you're vividly imagining with all your heart and all you soul and all your passion; it can't tell the difference between something that is actually happening. You get strong inside, you start thinking strong, and super emotional, and passionate about your goal. You reprogram yourself for success. You convince yourself you can hit your mark!"

Shakti Gawain

- "Imagination is the ability to create an idea, a mental picture, or a feeling sense of something. In creative visualization you use your imagination to create a clear image, idea, or feeling of something you wish to manifest. Then you continue to focus on the idea, feeling, or picture regularly, giving it positive energy until it becomes objective reality... in other words, until you actually achieve what you have been imagining. Your goal may be on any level — physical, emotional, mental, or spiritual."

USE VISUALIZATIONS TO TRAIN YOUR MIND TO ACCOMPLISH ANYTHING

- "We always attract into our lives whatever we think about the most, believe in most strongly, expect on the deepest levels, and/or imagine most vividly. When we are negative and fearful, insecure or anxious, we often attract the very experiences, situations, or people that we are seeking to avoid. If we are basically positive in attitude, expecting and envisioning pleasure, satisfaction, and happiness, we tend to attract and create people, situations, and events that conform to our positive expectations. So, consciously imagining what we want can help us to manifest it in our lives."

Steven Covey
- "Through imagination, we can visualize the uncreated worlds of potential that lie within us."

Zig Ziglar
- "If you can dream it, then you can achieve it."

53

Use Affirmations

To Fire-Up Your Positive Attitude

Jerry's Tips:

- An affirmation is a strong positive phrase you repeat to yourself that describes something you sincerely desire as already existing.

- An example of a short affirmation is: 'I am confident, I have a calm and alert mind, I radiate positive vibrations and people enjoy to be around me and to speak with me'.

- Affirmations are an important tool used for thousands of years to help people change negative aspects in their mind to become positive, and to boost their self-esteem and confidence.

- If you don't believe repetitive personal affirmations work as a way to get yourself to do something, remember that billions are spent on advertising and marketing to target your subconscious through repetition to 'sell you' to take action to buy or use their products and services. Why not learn how to 'sell yourself to yourself' to get what you want?

- Repeating affirmations provides positive vitamins for your mind.

- You can read an affirmation, but it's much more effective if you say it out loud because your voice infuses positive emotion into the affirmation.

- Saying an affirmation out loud plants the seed of a positive message in your mind which grows into positive thoughts, beliefs, attitudes, feelings and behaviors that counteract your negative self-talk.

USE AFFIRMATIONS TO FIRE-UP YOUR POSITIVE ATTITUDE

- An affirmation works if its message is believable to you, and you value the message and put emotional content and feeling in it when you repeat it.

- Like physical exercise, affirmations must be consistently used to produce maximum results.

- A good time to use an affirmation is when you wake up and before you go to sleep, and whenever you are feeling down or need a mental boost.

Jerry's Tips:

David J. Schwartz
- "Believe it can be done. When you believe something can be done, really believe, your mind will find the ways to do it. Believing a solution paves the way to solution."

Earl Nightingale
- "Whatever we plant in our subconscious mind and nourish with repetition and emotion will one day become a reality."

Emile Coue
- "Every day, in every way, I'm getting better and better."

Muhammad Ali
- "It's the repetition of affirmations that leads to belief. And once that belief becomes a deep conviction, things begin to happen."

- " 'I am the greatest,' I said that even before I knew I was."

- "Float like a butterfly sting like a bee."

Napoleon Hill
- "Any idea, plan, or purpose may be placed in the mind through repetition of thought."

Shakti Gawain
- "An affirmation is a strong, positive statement that something is already so."

W. Clement Stone
- "Self-suggestion makes you master of yourself."

54

Create And Celebrate Your Victory Journal

Jerry's Tips:

- Create a list of the experiences and accomplishments in your life that you greatly enjoyed and are very proud of. Carry that list with you and read it whenever you are feeling down. Vividly recall the feelings of happiness and success, and remind yourself that you have been a winner before, and that you have the power to win again!

- Remind yourself of past happiness and accomplishments to fire up your passion to accomplish, improve and be successful today and tomorrow.

Pat Croce

- "Like many goal-oriented individuals, I wouldn't think of starting my day without glancing at my day planner, reviewing my to-do list, and calculating the achievement of my daily game plan. But unlike most individuals, I supplement this preview with a review that makes all that work worthwhile. I call this my 'Victory Journal.'

It's basically a journal or diary filled with my handwritten account of personal and professional victories. Some victories are very subjective, and other victories are definitely objective. But as long as you perceive something to be a victory, then it's a victory and it deserves a place in your Victory Journal.

It can be anything from just a few keywords or simple sentences to a page-long overview of a particular achievement. The idea is to stimulate a mental reproduction of those special snapshots of success, which you can recall at a later date and savor for the rest of your life.

CREATE AND CELEBRATE YOUR VICTORY JOURNAL

Just like a photo album, your Victory Journal can become a great collection of snapshots of positive experiences and a living reminder of your power to achieve. And with such a clear record of all your daily wins, successes, triumphs, and achievements, you'll slowly build a strong sense of self-worth and a foundation for expecting success.

The Victory Journal can be especially useful when your attitude has twisted and soured, and as Zig Ziglar used to say, when your 'thinkin' becomes stinkin.' Or any time you're having a rotten day. Any committed optimist worth his or her weight in wisdom would admit that it's difficult to remain upbeat and positive when the critics and cynics are forecasting rain on your parade, or when you're tired or apprehensive, or when you've just suffered defeat or rejection.

In such times, one glance at the pages of your Victory Journal can be quite restorative. You quickly see that you have been a winner and realize that you can be a winner and you will be a winner again. I want you to post the following 4-line proverb where you can see it every day. In fact, tape it up right next to the picture that represents your vision.

Here it is:

Sow a thought, reap an action.
Sow an action, reap a habit.
Sow a habit, reap a character.
Sow a character, reap a destiny."

55

Communicate Effectively

Be Likeable, Connect, Establish Rapport And Build Trust To Get Your Message Across

Jerry's Tips:

- Go beyond merely communicating to 'connecting' with people.

- TRUST is the most important element for effective communication.

- Be likeable. People like to be with people they like.

- You don't get a second chance to make a first impression.

- Make a great first impression.

- Smile big – it instantly creates a positive relationship.

- Learn how to properly shake hands.

- Learn how to introduce yourself and others.

- People love to hear their own name. Learn to use it in conversation and treat it with respect.

- Call people by their names. When you call a person by their name they know you respect and value them.

- Be clear, brief, succinct, and to the point.

COMMUNICATE EFFECTIVELY
BE LIKEABLE, CONNECT, ESTABLISH RAPPORT AND BUILD TRUST TO GET YOUR MESSAGE ACROSS

- Learn to trade minds with other people. Always try to see through the eyes of the other person. What motivates them? What are they thinking about? What do they want? What would the other person think about what I am going to say or do? How would they react?

- Target your message for your particular audience.

- Put yourself in the other person's shoes.

- The biggest problem in communication is thinking you have clearly communicated without confirming it.

- Always make sure you have clearly communicated. Don't assume anything you said was clear. Ask for the other side to repeat it so both of you are sure.

- What you do speaks louder about who you are than what you say.

- The meaning of your communication is the response you get from the person you communicated with.

- Be empathetic, understand what people are feeling.

- Pause before you speak to show you are thinking about what the other person has said.

- Understand the use of verbal and non-verbal communication.

- Learn to really listen to what people say - verbally and non-verbally.

- We have two ears and one mouth because it's more important to listen than talk.

- Use reflective listening to confirm your understanding of what someone has said.

- Listen for what interests the person you are talking with and talk about it.

- Never interrupt anyone while they are speaking.

THE SUCCESS FORMULA FOR PERSONAL GROWTH

- Vary the speed of your voice.

- Learn how to tell a joke. People love to talk with people who can make them laugh.

- If you must disagree, disagree without being disagreeable.

- When someone says something you disagree with, tell them you value their point of view before you say anything contrary to it. This will make them receptive to what you say.

- When you give negative criticism wrap it in two slices of praise. First tell the person why you value them. Then explain what you think they did wrong or needs improvement. Then tell them you have confidence they will improve and be very successful.

- Don't hijack people's conversations. When you join a conversation talk about what they are talking about. Don't abruptly change the subject to what you want to talk about.

- Don't participate in negative gossip about people.

Abraham Lincoln
- "Everybody likes a compliment."

Ann Landers
- "Don't burden or depress those around you by dwelling on your minor aches and pains and small disappointments. Remember, everyone is carrying some kind of burden, often heavier than your own."

Benjamin Franklin
- "Remember not only to say the right thing in the right place, but far more difficult still, to leave unsaid the wrong thing at the tempting moment."

Bruce Lee
- "To know oneself is to study oneself in action with another person."

Communicate Effectively
Be likeable, connect, establish rapport and build trust to get your message across

Dale Carnegie
- "Speakers who talk about what life has taught them never fail to keep the attention of their listeners."

- "Tell the audience what you're going to say, say it; then tell them what you've said."

- "The only way to get the best of an argument is to avoid it."

- "The royal road to a man's heart is to talk to him about the things he treasures most."

- "Your purpose is to make your audience see what you saw, hear what you heard, feel what you felt. Relevant detail, couched in concrete, colorful language, is the best way to recreate the incident as it happened and to picture it for the audience."

- "When dealing with people, remember you are not dealing with creatures of logic, but creatures of emotion."

Ernest Hemingway
- "I like to listen. I have learned a great deal from listening carefully. Most people never listen."

Francois de La Rochefoucauld
- "To listen closely and reply well is the highest perfection we are able to attain in the art of conversation."

Henrik Ibsen
- "A thousand words will not leave so deep an impression as one deed."

Henry Ford
- "If there is any one secret of success, it lies in the ability to get the other person's point of view and see things from that person's angle as well as from your own."

Jim Rohn
- "The goal of effective communication should be for the listener to say, 'Me, too!' versus 'So what?'."

- "It's not the matter you cover so much as it is the manner in which you cover it."

- "Learn to express, not impress."

- "Be brief on the logic and reason portion of your presentation. There are probably about a thousand facts about an automobile, but you don't need them all to make a decision." About a half dozen will do."

- "One of the greatest gifts you can give to anyone is the gift of attention."

- "If you just communicate, you can get by. But if you communicate skillfully, you can work miracles."

- "Take advantage of every opportunity to practice your communication skills so that when important occasions arise, you will have the gift, the style, the sharpness, the clarity, and the emotions to affect other people."

John C. Maxwell
- "All things being equal people will do business with people they like. All things not being equal, they still will."

Lee Iacocca
- "You can have brilliant ideas, but if you can't get them across, your ideas won't get you anywhere."

Les Brown
- "Your ability to communicate is an important tool in your pursuit of your goals, whether it is with your family, your co-workers or your clients and customers."

- "To be an effective communicator you need to learn how to tell your story."

- "Never let what you want to say get in the way of what the audience needs to hear."

- "If you only talk to a person's head and not their heart people won't listen to you."

- "Once you open your mouth you tell the world who you are."

COMMUNICATE EFFECTIVELY
BE LIKEABLE, CONNECT, ESTABLISH RAPPORT AND BUILD TRUST TO GET YOUR MESSAGE ACROSS

Mae West
- "It's not what you say, but how you say it!"

Mark Twain
- "It is better to keep your mouth closed and let people think you are a fool than to open it and remove all doubt."

- "Action speaks louder than words but not nearly as often."

Napoleon Hill
- "Wise men, when in doubt whether to speak or to keep quiet, give themselves the benefit of the doubt, and remain silent."

- "Think twice before you speak, because your words and influence will plant the seed of either success or failure in the mind of another."

Norman Vincent Peale
- "Part of the happiness of life consists not in fighting battles but in avoiding them. A masterly retreat is in itself a victory."

Pat Croce
- "There are Six C's in Communication: Clear, Concise, Consistent, Credible, Courteous and Current."

Peter Drucker
- "The most important thing in communication is hearing what isn't said."

Plato
- "Wise men talk because they have something to say; fools, because they have to say something."

Steven Covey
- "Seek first to understand, then to be understood."

Thomas Jefferson
- "The most valuable of all talents is that of never using two words when one will do."

THE SUCCESS FORMULA FOR PERSONAL GROWTH

Tony Robbins
- "The way we communicate with others and with ourselves ultimately determines the quality of our lives."

- "Your level of communication mastery will determine your level of success with others, personally, emotionally, socially and financially."

- "To effectively communicate, we must realize that we are all different in the way we perceive the world and use this understanding as a guide to our communication with others."

Will Rogers
- "You never get a second chance to make a first impression."

- "After eating an entire bull, a mountain lion felt so good he started roaring. He kept it up until a hunter came along and shot him. The moral: When you're full of bull, keep your mouth shut."

Zig Ziglar
- "When you choose to be pleasant and positive in the way you treat others, you have also chosen, in most cases, how you are going to get treated by others."

- "What comes out of your mouth is determined by what goes into your mind."

56

Persuasion And Sales

All Communication Involves Selling Yourself And Your Ideas To Others

(Note: Please read the previous Chapter about how to *Communicate Effectively* before reading this Chapter.")

Jerry's Tips:

- Everyone is a salesperson whether they realize it or not. You may not be selling a product or service for money, but in our daily lives each of us are in situations where we need to influence and persuade other people and affect their decisions in favor of our position.

- Before someone will be persuaded by you, they must trust you, respect you, believe you are very knowledgeable in the subject, and that you are interested in finding out what their interests and needs are, and are 'suggesting' to them - not selling – the best solution to get the result they want or solve their need or problem.

- Do not view yourself as a salesperson or project to others that you are a salesperson when pitching anything. Instead, see and project yourself as a trusted advisor.

- Before you can persuade someone you must learn what they need, want or like and why.

- To be successful when you speak to persuade someone to do something, you must convey to the other person 'what's in it for them.' Explain the benefits to them of what you are presenting.

- Don't think of making a one time sale to someone. Instead, think how you can create a long term relationship with them which will result in repeat business and referals.

- Get the other person comfortable with saying 'yes' a few times to unimportant things before you ask them to commit to your main idea, proposal or what you are selling.

- The main ingredient to sell anything is to be enthusiastic about what you are selling! Your goal is to transfer your enthusiasm into the other person so they also feel enthusiastic to agree with you.

Abraham Lincoln
- "If you wish to win a man over to your ideas, first make him your friend."

Aristotle
- "Rhetoric = the ability to persuade."

Aristotle Onassis
- "To succeed in business it is necessary to make others see things as you see them."

Benjamin Franklin
- "If you would persuade, you must appeal to interest rather than intellect."

Bo Bennett
- "An objection is not a rejection; it is simply a request for more information."

Cavett Robert
- "People are persuaded more by the depth of your conviction than by the height of your logic – more by your own enthusiasm than any proof you can offer."

- "Persuasion is converting people – no, not to our way of thinking but to our way of feeling and believing."

Dale Carnegie
- "There is only one way to get anybody to do anything. And that is by making the other person want to do it."

PERSUASION AND SALES
ALL COMMUNICATION INVOLVES SELLING YOURSELF AND YOUR IDEAS TO OTHERS

- "Those convinced against their will are of the same opinion still."

- "When dealing with people, remember you are not dealing with creatures of logic, but creatures of emotion."

Dean Rusk
- "One of the best ways to persuade others is with your ears - by listening to them."

Frank Bettger
- "Show people what they want most, and they will move heaven and earth to get it."

John Hancock
- "The greatest ability in business is to get along with others and to influence their actions."

Laurence J. Peter
- "A man convinced against his will is not convinced."

Les Brown
- "Find out who the audience is and craft a message for 'them' from their point of view. It will determine whether you can persuade and close that person."

- "You want to have a strategic message so that after you've spoken to people, they will do more, perform differently, than they would have done had they not spoken to you."

Lyndon B. Johnson
- "What convinces is conviction. Believe in the argument you're advancing. If you don't you're as good as dead. The other person will sense that something isn't there, and no chain of reasoning, no matter how logical or elegant or brilliant, will win your case for you."

Michael Korda
- "It may be true that beauty is only skin-deep, but the fact reamins that the world judges you on your appearance a great deal of the time. It will hardly help your rise to success if you look like a loser. If you're going to be a winner, you may as well begin by looking like one."

Og Mandino
- "The image you project, in many circumstances, is far more valuable than your skills or your record of past accomplishments."

Tony Alessandra
- "To presuade or sell you must solve a person's problem or help them seize an opportunity."

Zig Ziglar
- "Selling is a transference of feeling."

- "The most important persuasion tool you have in your entire arsenal is integrity."

- "People don't buy for logical reasons, they buy for emotional reasons."

- "If people like you they'll listen to you, but if they trust you they'll do business with you."

57

Be Assertive When Necessary, Ask For And Say What You Want, Stick Up For Yourself

Jerry's Tips:

- In life you rarely get what you don't ask for.

- There is nothing wrong with asking for what you want or saying what you don't want.

- If you don't tell people what you want they won't know.

- Don't let anyone bully you into submission or silence. Find the power within you and stick up for yourself.

Anonymous
- "If you don't stick up for yourself, no one is going to do it for you."

Donald Trump
- "When somebody challenges you, fight back. Be brutal, be tough. Just go get them."

Harvey Fierstein
- "Never be bullied into silence. Never allow yourself to be made a victim."

Mohandas Gandhi
- "A 'No' uttered from the deepest conviction is better than a 'Yes' merely uttered to please, or worse, to avoid trouble."

Peter McWilliams
- "Learn to ask for what you want. The worst people can do is not give you what you ask for which is precisely where you were before you asked."

58

Build Your Personal Network

Jerry's Tips:

- Your personal growth and success is tied to your ability to build a network of people who you can look to for help and advice.

- To build a network, always think of how you can help other people in your network. People like to help people who help them.

- If you don't have a network of contacts ask yourself why? And ask yourself what you may be doing wrong? Then, make a plan and take action to start building your network.

- Don't think it's enough to just do your job at work. Attend company events and join industry associations – make it your job to meet and create a positive relationship with as many people as you can who can help you in your career.

- Practice how to introduce yourself and how to succinctly explain what you do, to put your best foot forward and capture the interest of the person you are talking with.

- If you attend a networking event stand where people can see and meet you. Don't hide in the corners.

Anonymous
- "It's not what you know but who you know that makes the difference."

Armstrong Williams
- "Networking is an essential part of building wealth."

Build Your Personal Network

Bob Burg
- "The successful networkers I know, the ones receiving tons of referrals and feeling truly happy about themselves, continually put the other person's needs ahead of their own."

- "It isn't just what you know, and it isn't just who you know. It's actually who you know, who knows you, and what you do for a living."

Mike Davidson
- "It's all about people. It's about networking and being nice to people and not burning any bridges."

Peter Drucker
- "More business decisions occur over lunch and dinner than at any other time, yet no MBA courses are given on the subject."

Tom Peters
- "Rolodex power. Your power is almost directly proportional to the thickness of your Rolodex, and the time you spend maintaining it. Put bluntly, the most potent people I've known have been the best networkers -- they 'know everybody from everywhere' and have just been out to lunch with most of them."

59

Treat Everyone Like A Customer, Provide World Class Service

Jerry's Tips:

- The better you treat people the more they will want to help you achieve your goals.

- Customers don't expect you and your product or service to be perfect. But they do expect you to quickly fix things when they have a problem.

- No one says a bad word about the person who gives them great service.

- Successful businesses know that lasting success requires providing great service to their customers so they stick with you and provide referrals. Apply this same lesson to your life. Value everyone you meet. You never know when they can help you, or say something good or bad about you to other people that can help or hurt your ability to achieve a goal and succeed.

- If you sell anything on the Internet, you must remember that your competitor is only a mouse click away.

- Treat your current customers so good that they will never become someone else's new customers.

- It's not enough to 'satisfy' your customers. You must provide exceptional service so they provide repeat referrals.

- Never take your friends, co-workers, loved ones or customers for granted. Thank them often, let them know they are valued and appreciated, and make them believe you are sincere.

- Treat each customer as if they are your only customer.

TREAT EVERYONE LIKE A CUSTOMER, PROVIDE WORLD CLASS SERVICE

Alice Foote Macdougall
- "In business you get what you want by giving other people what they want."

Anonymous
- "The Customer is King."

- "If we don't take care of our customers, someone else will."

- "To my customer:
  I may not have the answer, but I'll find it.
  I may not have the time, but I'll make it."

Benjamin Franklin
- "Well done is better than well said."

David J. Schwartz
- "Always give people more than they expect."

Jeff Bezos
- "If you make customers unhappy in the physical world, they might each tell 6 friends. If you make customers unhappy on the Internet, they can each tell 6,000 friends."

Jim Rohn
- "One good customer well taken care of could be more valuable than $10,000 worth of advertising."

- "If you make a sale you make a living. If you make an investment of time and good service in a customer, you can make a fortune."

Marshall Field
- "Goodwill is the only asset that competition cannot undersell or destroy."

Nelson Boswell
- "Here is a simple but powerful rule - always give people more than what they expect to get."

THE SUCCESS FORMULA FOR PERSONAL GROWTH

Peter Drucker
- "The purpose of business is to create and keep a customer."

- "Quality in a service or product is not what you put into it. It is what the client or customer gets out of it."

Sam Walton
- "The goal as a company is to have customer service that is not just the best, but legendary."

Tom Peters
- "Formula for success: under promise and over deliver."

Walt Disney
- "Do what you do so well that they will want to see it again and bring their friends."

60

Master Your Elevator Pitch And Personal Brand To Stand Out And Differentiate Yourself

Jerry's Tips:

- Your 'Elevator Pitch' is an expression that represents how, in 30 to 60 seconds, you can verbally present yourself and whatever product or service you personally provide or represent, to someone, with the goal to get them interested and excited to learn more about you and your product or service.

- To be effective your 'Elevator Pitch' should contain the following:
  1. What is the product or service you provide?
  2. Why does it exist?
  3. Who does it exist for?
  4. How do you have the expertise to provide this product or service?
  5. What value does it provide? What problem is solved by your product or service?

- Your Personal Brand is what people associate with you when they think about you. For instance, do they think you are an excellent salesperson or accountant? Is your reputation that you are very reliable and always keep your appointments? You must work to develop a personal brand and reputation that defines you in people's minds the way you want to be known.

Pamela Anderson
- "I'm not an actress. I don't think I am an actress. I think I've created a brand and a business."

THE SUCCESS FORMULA FOR PERSONAL GROWTH

Tom Peters
"Regardless of age, regardless of position, regardless of the business we happen to be in, all of us need to understand the importance of branding. We are CEOs of our own companies: Me Inc. To be in business today, our most important job is to be head marketer for the brand called You."

61

Teamwork

You Must Work Well And Get Along With People To Accomplish Your Goals

Jerry's Tips:

- At some point, no matter what you do you will need to work with other people to accomplish some part of your goals. Your ability to work effectively with other people will determine whether you succeed or fail.

- Our attitudes are infectious. If we work with people we must transmit positive attitudes to have a positive working relationship.

- Develop effective relationships with other people.

- Teamwork is the ability for two or more people to think 'we' instead of 'me' when they work toward a common goal.

- Teamwork works best when people like each other, respect each other, and they share a common interest that what they do together must and will succeed.

- Investing effort and time to improving teamwork is one of the best ways to improve a team's effectiveness and their likelihood to succeed with their individual and common goals.

Anonymous
- "Teamwork divides the task and multiplies the success."

- "It is amazing how much you can accomplish when it doesn't matter who gets the credit."

Babe Ruth
- "The way a team plays as a whole determines its success. You may have the greatest bunch of individual stars in the world, but if they don't play together, the club won't be worth a dime."

Brian Tracy
- "Teamwork is so important that it is virtually impossible for you to reach the heights of your capabilities or make the money that you want without becoming very good at it."

Dale Carnegie
- "You can close more business in two months by becoming interested in other people than you can in two years by trying to get people interested in you."

David J. Schwartz
- "Success depends on the support of other people. To get their support think right towards them and they will like and support you."

- "Think first class about everyone around you, and you'll receive first-class results in return."

- "People do more for you when you make them feel important."

- "When you help others feel important, you help yourself feel important too."

- "The big thinker always adds value to people by visualizing them at their best."

Earl Nightingale
- "Everything in the world we want to do or get done, we must do with and through people."

- "Our attitude towards others determines their attitude towards us."

Jim Rohn
- "You cannot succeed by yourself. It's hard to find a rich hermit."

TEAMWORK
YOU MUST WORK WELL AND GET ALONG WITH PEOPLE TO ACCOMPLISH YOUR GOALS

John Donne
- "No man is an island."

Henry Ford
- "Coming together is a beginning. Keeping together is progress. Working together is success."

Magic Johnson
- "Ask not what your teammates can do for you. Ask what you can do for your teammates."

Michael Jordan
- "Talent wins games, but teamwork and intelligence wins championships."

Pat Croce
- "Anything can be worked out, between anyone, at anytime, when you want the outcome bad enough."

Pat Riley
- "Great teamwork is the only way we create the breakthroughs that define our careers."

Theodore Roosevelt
- "The most important single ingredient to the formula of success is knowing how to get along with people."

Vince Lombardi
- "Individual commitment to a group effort - that is what makes a team work, a company work, a society work, a civilization work."
- "People who work together will win, whether it be against complex football defenses, or the problems of modern society."
- "The achievements of an organization are the results of the combined effort of each individual."

Yogi Berra
- "When you're part of a team, you stand up for your teammates. Your loyalty is to them. You protect them through good and bad, because they'd do the same for you."

62

Leadership

Respect And Value People To Inspire Them To Do Their Best

Jerry's Tips:

- The skills of an effective leader to lead other people can be used to operate a successful business, and you can use the same skills to lead and create a successful personal life.

- When you think about individual business skills, think how they can be applied in your own life, for example, planning and goal setting, marketing and team building.

- You must be the captain of your own ship to lead yourself and others to success.

- Leadership is performed by two types of leaders: those who have a leadership title and everyone else in the world.

- Self-Leadership is having an internal compass that sets your direction for every move you make each day.

- We are all leaders of our own lives.

- Don't be a run-of-the-mill manager of your life; Be a visionary leader with goals and a plan to achieve them.

- Think like a CEO to lead your life. Think return on investment (ROI) of your time and resources, increase your capacity, skills and productivity, and market your personal brand.

- Top notch leaders know that effective leaders are likeable; though that doesn't mean they are soft.

LEADERSHIP
RESPECT AND VALUE PEOPLE
TO INSPIRE THEM TO DO THEIR BEST

- Don't be a dictator that rules people by force or fear. People follow dictators but they will never give them 100% of their support, and none of their creativity.

- The authoritative command leader is never as effective as the coach leader. A leader who always blames people under their supervision for mistakes, or tells other leaders in the organization, or their own boss, that those under their supervision are stupid for making so many mistakes, has missed the point that a leader is supposed to take personal responsibility for all mistakes and blame only themselves.

- The most important skills to be a leader are: Lead by example, know how to recruit and get the best from each person, know how to build high performing teams, have an open mind, and know how to teach people to think in new directions.

- Great leaders know how to instill pride in the people who work for them, to be proud of the work they do.

- Don't ever refer to people working with or for you as 'human resources.' People like to be treated like 'people,' not 'resources' such as a desk, chair or a computer.

- An excellent leader makes people feel valued and empowered.

- Some leaders never say a sincere 'thank you'. A real leader knows that saying 'thank you' and making those under their supervision feel appreciated, valued and empowered are the most important things a leader can do. Otherwise, given the opportunity people will eventually leave.

- Unfortunately, many leaders don't have people skills and are not real coaches even if they think they are. Talk about metrics and process all day long (they are important), however, in the end 'people' perform the processes, and a leader better know how to make people feel appreciated, or the process will not be effective.

- A brilliant business process cannot truly succeed unless you inspire the people who perform it to get along and think about the value of helping each other like family. That's real leadership.

THE SUCCESS FORMULA FOR PERSONAL GROWTH

- A leader must be quick to spot problems and take action to find solutions.

- Lay the law down that everyone in your company must be fully prepared to attend all of their meetings, arrive on time, not waste time in meetings, and perform their responsibilities and assignments when due.

- Great leaders don't hoard knowledge. They know that knowledge is like peanut butter, it works best when spread around.

- Excellent leaders know that you can't do everything yourself - delegate, delegate, delegate.

- For leaders to be most useful to their company, and to the productivity of the people they supervise, leaders must make the people they supervise feel that they are approachable, and welcome new ideas, criticism and questions from them.

Anonymous
- "A word of encouragement during a failure is worth more than an hour of praise after success."

Andrew Carnegie
- "No man will make a great leader who wants to do it all himself or get all the credit for doing it."

Arnold H. Glasow
- "A leader has the ability to recognize a problem before it becomes an emergency."

Bill Bradley
- "Leadership is unlocking people's potential to become better."

Charles Schwab
- "I have yet to find the man, however exalted his station, who did not do better work and put forth greater effort under a spirit of approval than under a spirit of criticism."

LEADERSHIP
RESPECT AND VALUE PEOPLE
TO INSPIRE THEM TO DO THEIR BEST

- "I consider my ability to arouse enthusiasm among men the greatest asset I possess. The way to develop the best that is in a man is by appreciation and encouragement."

Dwight D. Eisenhower

- "Leadership is the art of getting someone to do something you want done because he wants to do it."

General Douglas MacArthur

General MacArthur was a brilliant strategist and a farsighted administrator. He developed a list of questions to guide him in his leadership duties. The principles in these questions can be applied to any leadership situation.

- "Do I heckle my subordinates or strengthen and encourage them?

    Do I use moral courage in getting rid of subordinates who have proven themselves beyond doubt to be unfit?

    Have I done all in my power by encouragement, incentive and spur to salvage the weak and erring?

    Do I know by NAME and CHARACTER a maximum number of subordinates for whom I am responsible?

    Do I know them intimately?

    Am I thoroughly familiar with the technique, necessities, objectives and administration of my job?

    Do I lose my temper at individuals?

    Do I act in such a way as to make my subordinates WANT to follow me?

    Do I delegate tasks that should be mine?

    Do I arrogate everything to myself and delegate nothing?

    Do I develop my subordinates by placing on each one as much responsibility as he can stand?

THE SUCCESS FORMULA FOR PERSONAL GROWTH

Am I interested in the personal welfare of each of my subordinates, as if he were a member of my family?

Have I the calmness of voice and manner to inspire confidence, or am I inclined to irascibility and excitability?

Am I a constant example to my subordinates in character, dress, deportment and courtesy?

Am I inclined to be nice to my superiors and mean to my subordinates?

Is my door open to my subordinates?

Do I think more of POSITION than JOB?

Do I correct a subordinate in front of others?"

General George S. Patton
- "Be willing to make decisions. That's the most important quality in a good leader."

- "Issuing orders is worth about 10 percent. The remaining 90 percent consists in assuring proper and vigorous execution of the order."

- "If everyone is thinking alike, then someone isn't thinking."

- "Never tell people how to do things. Tell them what to do and they will surprise you with their ingenuity."

Howard Schultz
- "Treat people like family, and they will be loyal and give their all. Stand by people, and they will stand by you. It's the oldest formula in business, one that is second nature to many family-run firms."

Jack Welch
- "Giving people self-confidence is by far the most important thing that I can do. Because then they will act."

Jeffrey Immelt
- "Every leader needs to clearly explain the top three things the organization is working on. If you can't, you are not leading well."

LEADERSHIP
RESPECT AND VALUE PEOPLE
TO INSPIRE THEM TO DO THEIR BEST

Jim Rohn
- "Lead the way by personal example and by personal philosophy."

- "The challenge of leadership is to be strong, but not rude; be kind, but not weak; be bold, but not bully; be thoughtful, but not lazy; be humble, but not timid; be proud, but not arrogant; have humor, but without folly."

John Quincy Adams
- "If your actions inspire others to dream more, learn more, do more and become more, you are a leader."

Napoleon Bonaparte
- "A leader is a dealer in hope."

Peter Drucker
- "Management is doing things right; leadership is doing the right things."

Philip Armour
- "No general can fight his battles alone. He must depend upon his lieutenants, and his success depends upon his ability to select the right man for the right place."

Ray Kroc
- "The quality of a leader is reflected in the standards they set for themselves."

Robert Collier
- "Most of us, swimming against the tides of trouble the world knows nothing about, need only a bit of praise or encouragement - and we will make the goal."

Russell H. Ewing
- "A boss creates fear, a leader confidence. A boss fixes blame, a leader corrects mistakes. A boss knows all, a leader asks questions. A boss makes work drudgery, a leader makes it interesting."

THE SUCCESS FORMULA FOR PERSONAL GROWTH

Sam Walton
- "Outstanding leaders go out of their way to boost the self-esteem of their personnel. If people believe in themselves, it's amazing what they can accomplish."

Tom Peters
- "The simple act of paying positive attention to people has a great deal to do with productivity."

- "Leaders don't create followers, they create more leaders."

Steve Bennett
- "The essential skills and characteristics of a top leader are:

    1. **Have the courage to use judgment.**
    Business rules never substitute for judgment, and business decisions are almost never black and white. Ninety-five percent of business decisions require qualitative assessment.

    2. **Prioritize how you spend your time.**
    Great leaders understand that time is an investment, not an expense. Combining their skills with the proper allocation of their time, on the right priorities, is critical for leadership success.

    3. **Build strong teams.**
    A leader should have high standards for hiring employees—then the leader should grow their talent by teaching them how to fish, not by feeding them."

Tony Blair
- "The art of leadership is saying no, not yes. It is very easy to say yes."

Vince Lombardi
- "A leader must identify himself with the group, must back up the group, even at the risk of displeasing superiors. He must believe that the group wants from him a sense of approval. If this feeling prevails, production, discipline, morale will be high, and in return, you can demand the cooperation to promote the goals of the company."

- "Leadership is based on a spiritual quality; the power to inspire, the power to inspire others to follow."

LEADERSHIP
RESPECT AND VALUE PEOPLE
TO INSPIRE THEM TO DO THEIR BEST

Voltaire
- "Think for yourselves and let others enjoy the privilege to do so, too."

63

Don't Waste Your Time Or Let Anyone Else Waste It, Be Organized And Prioritize

Jerry's Tips:

- Time is life. When you run out of time you run out of life.

- Stop living your life as if you have a thousand years to live and become successful – You don't! Hurry up and make something of your life before you run out of time!

- Treasure and use each precious minute of your time as if it were the last minute you have.

- The value of your time is priceless, but unfortunately it's not until you have reached your end that you realize its worth.

- The biggest mistake you can make in life is to waste your time.

- Having a happy and enjoyable life where you are able to provide for yourself, your family and loved ones, help your friends and the larger community, requires you to become the best you can be in life. You must use your time as effectively and efficiently to develop yourself into a person with a successful life, or else you might run out of time to do so.

- It's easy to sleep all day. You must get up and take positive action in service of your goals to be successful.

- Do not sleep your way through life. Wake up! Live the time you have! Make something out of yourself with your time here or get used to big disappointments in life.

- Invest your time, don't just use it.

DON'T WASTE YOUR TIME OR LET ANYONE ELSE WASTE IT, BE ORGANIZED AND PRIORITIZE

- Before you start to spend time doing something ask yourself 'What benefit are you going to get from doing that activity? Is there a better use of your time?'

- Get in the habit of asking yourself: 'Is what I am doing, this minute, moving me closer to my major goals?'

- The reason so many people are not successful is because they spend too much time on their secondary activities, time wasters and hobbies, that they don't have time to perform work that will get them where they want to go in life.

- You must manage your time and not just use it.

- First things first, everything you do is done better when it's organized.

- You must prioritize what you do because there are always more things to do than there is time to do them.

- Make a prioritized To-Do list and always keep it with you.

- Always know what your top 3 priorities are, and do something every day to accomplish them.

- Prioritize your most important tasks and work on your higher priority tasks before working on your lower priority tasks.

- Focus on 'important' tasks and do not get caught up spending too much time on any 'urgent' tasks that are not important.

- Have a sense of last minute urgency all the time. This means focus and work as hard on a task at the beginning of the task, and whenever you work on it, as if you were running out of time to complete it.

- Invest some time to prevent future problems.

- Spend some time every day on a task to accomplish your goal, this chips away at it and keeps it fresh in your mind. Don't skip days working on a goal or you may stop working on the task.

- Focus on one thing at a time.

THE SUCCESS FORMULA FOR PERSONAL GROWTH

- Multitasking is evil. But know how to chew gum and walk at the same time.

- It is preferable to do one thing at a time and do it superbly, with all your concentration and skill. However, there are times when we must know how to do more than one thing at a time, such as walking and talking or driving a car while tuning its radio.

- Unless required for your work, never say 'Yes' to spending your time with someone or doing something they ask you to do unless you really want to do it. Learn to say 'No' to activities and people that will waste your time.

- Most people get fatigued and cannot work effectively for long periods of time. Use 'timeboxing' which means to work in short controlled bursts to perform your tasks at a sustained optimal level.

- Work in short blocks of time, 15 minutes, 30 minutes, take a break, continue… Whatever tempo works best for you.

- Use a timer to make sure you don't work too long or too short.

- Be punctual. Never be late. 1 hour early is better than 5 minutes late for an appointment with someone. Being on time shows respect for yourself and others. Don't steal other people's time by being late.

- Turn off the TV and turn on your life!

- Maximize your time. Einstein worked on his breakthrough theories while working as a clerk in the Patent Office.

- Don't confuse rushing or being busy with being productive or effective. Many people are very frantically busy but don't accomplish much that is really important.

- Spend as much time as you can with your children and use that time to let them know they are loved and important, and that they can learn to do and become anything they want to, if they are willing to work hard for it.

DON'T WASTE YOUR TIME OR LET ANYONE ELSE WASTE IT, BE ORGANIZED AND PRIORITIZE

Anonymous
- "If you waste time, time will waste you."
- "Don't count time. Make time count."
- "We are too busy mopping the floor to turn off the faucet."
- "We all have the same amount of time. It's just a matter of what we do with it."
- "If everything is a top priority, then nothing is a top priority – You must rank your priorities."

Benjamin Franklin
- "Lost time is never found again."
- "Do not squander time for that is the stuff life is made of."
- "Employ thy time well, if thou meanest to gain leisure."
- "You may delay, but time will not, and lost time is never found again."
- "Never leave that till tomorrow which you can do today."
- "Time is money."

Bill Gates
- "I always ask: 'Am I doing the things that are the most important?'"

Bo Bennett
- "Every minute you spend in your life is either spent bringing you closer to your goals or moving you away from your goals."

Brian Tracy
- "If what you are doing is not moving you towards your goals, then it's moving you away from your goals."
- "If you love life, don't waste time, for time is what life is made up of."

C. Northcote Parkinson
- "Parkinson's Law: Work expands so as to fill the time available for its completion."

Charles Darwin
- "A man who dares to waste one hour of time has not discovered the value of life."

Dan Kennedy
- "Productivity is the deliberate, strategic investment of your time, talent, intelligence, energy, resources and opportunities in a manner calculated to move you measurably closer to meaningful goals."

- "By reducing unscheduled time and unplanned activity, you automatically reduce waste."

Etienne de Grellet
- "I shall pass through this life but once. Any good therefore that I can do, or any kindness I can show, let me do it now. Let me not defer or neglect it. For I shall never pass this way again."

Francis Bacon
- "Begin doing what you want to do now. We are not living in an eternity. We have only this moment, sparkling like a star in our hand – and melting like a snowflake."

H. Jackson Brown, Jr.
- "Don't say you don't have enough time. You have exactly the same number of hours per day that were given to Helen Keller, Pasteur, Michelangelo, Mother Teresa, Leonardo Da Vinci, Thomas Jefferson, and Albert Einstein."

Henry Ford
- "It has been my observation that most people get ahead during the time that others waste."

- "Most people spend more time and energy going around problems than in trying to solve them."

Jim Rohn
- "Time is more valuable than money. You can get more money, but you cannot get more time."

DON'T WASTE YOUR TIME OR LET ANYONE ELSE WASTE IT, BE ORGANIZED AND PRIORITIZE

- "Days are expensive. When you spend a day, you have one less day to spend. So make sure you spend each one wisely."

- "Make rest a necessity, not an objective. Only rest long enough to gather strength."

- "Either you run the day or the day runs you."

- "Learn how to separate the majors and the minors. A lot of people don't do well simply because they major in minor things."

- "We can no more afford to spend major time on minor things than we can to spend minor time on major things."

- "Time is our most valuable asset, yet we tend to waste it, kill it, and spend it, rather than invest it."

Lee Iacocca
- "If you want to make good use of your time, you've got to know what's most important and then give it all you've got."

Louisa May Alcott
- "Make each day useful and cheerful and prove that you know the worth of time by employing it well. Then youth will be happy, old age without regret and life a beautiful success."

Marcus Aurelius
- "Do not act as if you had a thousand years to live."

- "How much time he saves who does not look to see what his neighbor says or does or thinks."

- "Waste no more time talking about great souls and how they should be. Become one yourself!"

Mark Twain
- "One thing at a time, is my motto - and just play that thing for all it is worth, even if it's only two pair and a jack."

Michael LeBoeuf
- "Waste your money and you're only out of money, but waste your time and you've lost a part of your life."

THE SUCCESS FORMULA FOR PERSONAL GROWTH

- "The ultimate goal of a more effective and efficient life is to provide you with enough time to enjoy some of it."

Og Mandino
- "This day is all you have and these hours are now your eternity. Greet this sunrise with cries of joy as a prisoner who is reprieved from death."

- "Grasp each minute of this day with both hands and fondle it with love for its value is beyond price."

Orison Swett Marden
- "People do not realize the immense value of utilizing spare minutes."

Pat Croce
- "Apply the 4 "D" system to every item that crosses your desktop: Do it now! Delegate it. Defer it (file it). Or Discard it."

- "The basic purpose of a 'to-do' list is to help you remember to follow through on something you committed to or would like to get done. The problem is when you sit down to create a 'to-do' list all the items you think of, regardless of when they have to be completed, often all appear on one giant list.

    These giant 'to-do' lists often make us feel overwhelmed, frustrated, trapped and less productive rather than more productive. The most basic function of a day planner is to act as a 365-day 'to-do' list. Instead of having one giant, hope you lose it and never find it again list, you have 365 little manageable ones that keep you focused and productive."

- "What is the hardest action step on your to-do list today? Attack it right now!"

Patrick Dixon
- "Life is too short to waste on things that don't matter."

Peter Drucker
- "Time is the scarcest resource and unless it is managed nothing else can be managed."

DON'T WASTE YOUR TIME OR LET ANYONE ELSE WASTE IT, BE ORGANIZED AND PRIORITIZE

Robert G. Allen
- "Routine brings results. A disorganized genius is no match for the average person with a daily routine."

Robin S. Sharma
- "Time slips through our hands like grains of sand, never to return again."

Russian Proverb
- "If you chase two rabbits, you catch neither."

Saint Ignatius Loyola
- "He who does well one work at a time, does more than all."

Samuel Smiles
- "Some take no thought of the value of money until they have come to an end of it, and many do the same with their time. The hours are allowed to flow by unemployed, and then, when life is fast waning, they bethink themselves of the duty of making a wiser use of it. But the habit of listlessness and idleness may already have become confirmed, and they are unable to break the bonds with which they have permitted themselves to become bound. Lost wealth may be replaced by industry, lost knowledge by study, lost health by temperance or medicine, but lost time is gone for ever."

Steven Covey
- "You have to decide what your highest priorities are and have the courage - pleasantly, smilingly, non-apologetically - to say 'no' to other things."

- "Keep in mind that you are always saying 'no' to something. If it isn't to the apparent, urgent things in your life, it is probably to the most fundamental, highly important things. Even when the urgent is good, the good can keep you from your best, keep you from your unique contribution, if you let it."

- "The key is not to prioritize what's on your schedule, but to schedule your priorities."

- "The main thing is to keep the main thing the main thing."

THE SUCCESS FORMULA FOR PERSONAL GROWTH

Tony Robbins
- "Once you have mastered time, you will understand how true it is that most people overestimate what they can accomplish in a year - and underestimate what they can achieve in a decade!"

Vilfredo Pareto
- "The 80-20 Rule: 80% of your important results are produced by 20% of what you do so concentrate on the most important things."

Zig Ziglar
- "Remember, you can earn more money, but when time is spent it is gone forever."

64

Learn From Your Past, Live In The Present, Plan For Your Future

Jerry's Tips:

- Don't allow your present and future success to be consumed by your past.

- Don't hold on to the past so tightly that you don't have a free hand to embrace your future.

- Whether it is 10 years ago or yesterday, the past is gone, and you only have right now to live. Live in the moment.

- Don't carry around past disappointments and grudges. Let them go so you can live your life in the present to its fullest.

- If you keep looking back with one eye to an unhappy past you won't have two eyes to be able to see your bright future ahead.

- Make peace with your past.

- You must understand and learn from your past to live your best now and be able to plan for your future.

- Whatever you are doing right now, do it with all the attention, awareness and presence that you can muster. Don't let your life pass you by while you are thinking about something else that is a past shadow of your life.

Anonymous
- "Live in the present, not the past or future. We must learn from the past to plan for the future, but don't spend too much time there."

THE SUCCESS FORMULA FOR PERSONAL GROWTH

- "Learn from yesterday, live for today, hope for tomorrow."

- "Once you stop living in the past, you'll wake up to the world around you. The present is a pretty great place to be."

Babatunde Olatunji
- "Yesterday is history. Tomorrow is a mystery. And today? Today is a gift. That's why we call it the present."

Babe Ruth
- "Yesterday's home runs don't win today's games."

Bill Cosby
- "The past is a ghost, the future a dream, and all we ever have is now."

Buddha
- "The secret of health for both mind and body is not to mourn for the past, not to worry about the future, not to anticipate the future, but to live the present moment wisely and earnestly."

Cherokee Proverb
- "Don't let yesterday use up too much of today."

Denis Waitley
- "Losers live in the past. Winners learn from the past and enjoy working in the present toward the future."

- "Learn from the past, set vivid, detailed goals for the future, and live in the only moment of time over which you have any control: now."

Donald Trump
- "I try to learn from the past, but I plan for the future by focusing exclusively on the present. That's were the fun is."

Eckhart Tolle
- "Realize deeply that the present moment is all you ever have. Make the Now the primary focus of your life."

Henry Wadsworth Longfellow
- "The present is the blocks with which we build."

Johann Wolfgang von Goethe
- "Nothing is worth more than this day."

LEARN FROM YOUR PAST, LIVE IN THE PRESENT, PLAN FOR YOUR FUTURE

John Wooden
- "Don't look back. Look forward. You're not going to change anything. Learn from the past, but you're not going to change it. Nothing will change it. The future is yet to be. And, can you affect the future? Yes. How? By what you do every single day. Either consciously or subconsciously."

- "I've shut the door on yesterday, thrown the key away. Tomorrow holds no fears for me, for I have found today."

Mohandas Gandhi
- "The future depends on what we do in the present."

Oprah Winfrey
- "Breathe. Let go. And remind yourself that this very moment is the only one you know you have for sure."

Ronald Reagan
- "While I take inspiration from the past, like most Americans, I live for the future."

William Wordsworth
- "Life is divided into three terms - that which was, which is, and which will be. Let us learn from the past to profit by the present, and from the present to live better in the future."

65

Look For Opportunities And How To Take Advantage Of Them

Jerry's Tips:

- Think like an entrepreneur – always be on the lookout for opportunity and how to exploit it.

- Opportunities are all around you, if you have the courage to take the time to look for and pursue them.

- Most people don't recognize opportunity because it's frequently masked in failure, seems impossible to achieve, or looks like work.

- There is always a hidden opportunity in a problem if you look for it.

- You must have a mindset to always look for and create new opportunities. If a door closes look for another door that opens.

- If you lose a job, make sure you consider whether it might be a blessing in disguise, and an opportunity to work at something else you really want to do.

- The successful person recognizes opportunity, evaluates thier choices and makes decisive decisions that bring them closer to achieving their goals.

- Grasp quickly at an opportunity. It will not sit around and wait for you.

- Don't ignore small opportunities. They often lead to larger opportunities.

Look for Opportunities
and How to Take Advantage of Them

- To breakthrough or get to the next level, look around for opportunities - then climb the high board and take the jump. After you do you will be changed for life and it will be easier after you take the plunge.

Albert Einstein
- "In the middle of difficulty lies opportunity."

Alexander Graham Bell
- "When one door closes, another opens; but we often look so long and so regretfully upon the closed door that we do not see the one which has opened for us."

- "Sometimes we stare so long at a door that is closing that we see too late the one that is open."

Ayn Rand
- "The ladder of success is best climbed by stepping on the rungs of opportunity."

Benjamin Franklin
- "To succeed, jump as quickly at opportunities as you do at conclusions."

Charles R. Swindoll
- "We are all faced with a series of great opportunities brilliantly disguised as impossible situations."

Demosthenes
- "Small opportunities are often the beginning of great enterprises."

Frank Tyger
- "Learn to listen. Opportunity could be knocking at your door very softly."

Gloria Estefan
- "The sad truth is that opportunity doesn't knock twice. You can put things off until tomorrow but tomorrow may never come."

THE SUCCESS FORMULA FOR PERSONAL GROWTH

Jim Carrey
"Life opens up opportunities to you, and you either take them or you stay afraid of taking them."

Jim Rohn
"We must become sensitive enough to observe and ponder what is happening around us. Be alert. Be awake. Let life and all of its subtle messages touch us."

Jinger Heath
"Look for opportunity. You can't wait for it to knock on the door. ... you might not be home."

John Sculley
"The future belongs to those who see possibilities before they become obvious."

Lee Iacocca
"We are continually faced by great opportunities brilliantly disguised as insoluble problems."

Dr. Maxwell Maltz
"What is opportunity, and when does it knock? It never knocks. You can wait a whole lifetime, listening, hoping, and you will hear no knocking. None at all. You are opportunity, and you must knock on the door leading to your destiny. You prepare yourself to recognize opportunity, to pursue and seize opportunity as you develop the strength of your personality, and build a self-image with which you are able to live -- with your self-respect alive and growing."

Niccolo Machiavelli
"Entrepreneurs are simply those who understand that there is little difference between obstacle and opportunity and are able to turn both to their advantage."

Dr. Robert H. Schuller
"High achievers spot rich opportunities swiftly, make big decisions quickly and move into action immediately. Follow these principles and you can make your dreams come true."

Milton Berle
"If opportunity doesn't knock, build a door."

Look for Opportunities
and How to Take Advantage of Them

Napoleon Hill
- "Opportunity often comes disguised in the form of misfortune, or temporary defeat."

Rita Coolidge
- "Too often the opportunity knocks, but by the time you push back the chain, push back the bolt, unhook the locks and shut off the burglar alarm, it's too late."

Robert Collier
- "As fast as each opportunity presents itself, use it! No matter how tiny an opportunity it may be, use it!"

Samuel Smiles
- "Men who are resolved to find a way for themselves will always find opportunities enough; and if they do not find them, they will make them."

Sun Tzu
- "Opportunities multiply as they are seized."

Thomas Edison
- "The reason a lot of people do not recognize opportunity is because it usually disguises itself as hard work."

- "Opportunity is missed by most people because it is dressed in overalls and looks like work."

66

Have An Open Mind To New Ideas And Don't Let Ideas Escape

Jerry's Tips:

- Just because you know a way that works that doesn't mean there isn't a better way.

- It's impossible for a person to learn something if they already think they know it.

- Don't think you know everything.

- Be open minded, seek out and be receptive to new ideas.

- Good ideas can come from anyone, not just those with an impressive job title. Never ignore or discount an idea because the person who raises it does not have a lot of experience or a fancy job title.

- Ideas are lighter than helium. Capture ideas before they float away.

- When you have an idea, immediately write it down or save it somehow before it floats away and you can't remember it.

Albert Einstein
- "The mind that opens to a new idea never comes back to its original size."

- "Great ideas often receive violent opposition from mediocre minds."

Anonymous
- "The mind is like a parachute - it works only when it is open."

HAVE AN OPEN MIND TO NEW IDEAS AND DON'T LET IDEAS ESCAPE

David J. Schwartz
- "Become receptive to ideas. Welcome new ideas. Destroy these thought repellents: 'Won't work,' 'Can't be done,' 'It's useless,' and 'It's stupid.' "

- "Don't let ideas escape. ... Write them down. Every day lots of good ideas are born only to die quickly because they aren't nailed to paper."

- "Carry a notebook or some small cards with you. When you get an idea, write it down... People with fertile, creative minds know a good idea may sprout any time, any place. Don't let ideas escape; else you destroy the fruits of your thinking."

Earl Nightingale
- "You'll find boredom where there is the absence of a good idea."

Epictetus
- "It is impossible to begin to learn that which one thinks one already knows."

Gloria Steinem
- "The first problem for us all, men and women, is not to learn, but to unlearn."

Jim Rohn
- "Ideas can be life-changing. Sometimes all you need to open the door is just one more good idea."

- "Keep a journal. Don't trust your memory. When you listen to something valuable, write it down. When you come across something important, write it down."

Les Brown
- "Don't let tradition paralyze your mind. Be receptive to new ideas. Be experimental. Try new approaches. Be progressive in everything you do."

- "Get your ideas on paper and study them. Do not let them go to waste!"

THE SUCCESS FORMULA FOR PERSONAL GROWTH

Earl Nightingale
- "Ideas are elusive, slippery things. Best to keep a pad of paper and a pencil at your bedside, so you can stab them during the night before they get away."

Martha Stewart
- "Without an open-minded mind, you can never be a great success."

Richard Branson
- "I have always lived my life by thriving on opportunity and adventure. Some of the best ideas come out of the blue, and you have to keep an open mind to see their virtue."

67

Be Creative

Invent And Innovate, Look For New And Better Ways To Do Things

Jerry's Tips:

- Knowledge plus the creativity to use that knowledge in new and different ways is a formula for success.

- Doing what everyone else does may keep you in the game, but you'll only achieve great success if you are creative and figure out how to do something new or better.

- Creativity is a state of mind. You can choose to think creatively.

- To be creative, think how different concepts or existing products or services can relate to each other and compliment each other to produce something of value.

- Creativity is seeing how one of this plus one of that can equal three.

- There's value in looking for new and improved ways to do things.

- Look for synergies between things.

- Creativity is not just for artists. Everyone can be creative in whatever they do.

THE SUCCESS FORMULA FOR PERSONAL GROWTH

David J. Schwartz
- "The successful business man says 'What I want around me, are people who can solve problems, who can think up ideas. People who can dream and then develop the dream into a practical application; an idea man can make money with me, a fact man cannot.'"

- "Creative thinking is simply finding new, improved ways to do anything."

- "Einstein taught us a big lesson. He felt it was more important to use your mind to think than to use it as a warehouse of facts."

- "Top success is reserved for the I-can-do-it-better kind of persons. It works magic. When you ask yourself that how-can-I–do–it–better question, your creative power is switched on and ways for doings things better suggest themselves."

Dee Hock
- "The problem is never how to get new, innovative thoughts into your mind, but how to get old ones out."

Edwin Land
- "An essential aspect of creativity is not being afraid to fail."

Henry J. Heinz
- "To do a common thing uncommonly well brings success."

Irvine Robbins
- "You look at any giant corporation, and I mean the biggies, and they all started with a guy with an idea, doing it well."

J. Paul Getty
- "The man who comes up with a means for doing or producing almost anything better, faster or more economically has his future and his fortune at his fingertips."

Jim Rohn
- "There are only 3 colors, 10 digits, and 7 notes; it's what we do with them that's important."

- "If you wish to find, you must search. Rarely does a good idea interrupt you."

BE CREATIVE, INVENT AND INNOVATE
LOOK FOR NEW AND BETTER WAYS TO DO THINGS

Larry Ellison
- "When you innovate, you've got to be prepared for everyone telling you you're nuts."

Orville Wright
- "If we all worked on the assumption that what is accepted as true is really true, there would be little hope of advance."

Pat Croce
- "Imitation may keep you in the race, but it's innovation that will help win the race."

Roger Von Oech
- "Take advantage of the ambiguity in the world. Look at something and think what else it might be."

Russell Simmons
- "The imagination is how things get done. You have to cultivate creativity."

Thomas Edison
- "There's a way to do it better - find it."

68

Personal Character Counts

Jerry's Tips:

- Your Mother said it best when she told you: 'Treat people the way you would want them to treat you.'

- If you live your life by treating people good you will feel good.

Abigail Van Buren
- "The best index to a person's character is:
  1. how he treats people who can't do him any good, and
  2. how he treats people who can't fight back."

Abraham Lincoln
- "Reputation is the shadow. Character is the tree."

- "When I do good, I feel good; when I do bad, I feel bad. That's my religion."

Albert Einstein
- "Most people say that it is the intellect which makes a great scientist. They are wrong: it is character."

Anonymous
- "Good character is more to be praised than outstanding talent. Most talents are, to some extent, a gift. Good character, by contrast, is not given to us. We have to build it piece by piece -- by thought, choice, courage and determination."

Personal Character Counts

Confucius
- "What you do not want others to do to you, do not do to others."

Henry Kravis
- "If you don't have integrity, you have nothing. You can't buy it. You can have all the money in the world, but if you are not a moral and ethical person, you really have nothing."

Cherokee Indian Story
- "An old Cherokee was teaching his grandchildren about life.

    He said to them, 'A battle is raging inside me ... it is a terrible fight between two wolves.

    One wolf represents fear, anger, envy, sorrow, regret, greed, arrogance, self-pity, guilt, resentment, inferiority, lies, false pride, superiority and ego.

    The other stands for joy, peace, love, hope, sharing, serenity, humility, kindness, benevolence, friendship, empathy, generosity, truth, compassion and faith.'

    The old man fixed the children with a firm stare. 'This same fight is going on inside you, and inside every other person, too.'

    They thought about it for a minute and then one child asked his grandfather, 'Which wolf will win?'

    The old Cherokee replied: 'The one you feed.' "

Jesus Christ
- "Do unto others as you would have them do unto you."

John Wooden
- "Be more concerned with your character than your reputation, because your character is what you really are, while your reputation is merely what others think you are."

Les Brown
- "Don't judge people by what they do. Judge people by what they do that they don't have to."

THE SUCCESS FORMULA FOR PERSONAL GROWTH

- "Character may be manifested in the great moments, but it is made in the small ones."

Martin Luther King, Jr.
- "The ultimate measure of a man is not where he stands in moments of comfort, and convenience, but where he stands at times of challenge and controversy."

Pat Riley
- "The Ten Commandments were not a suggestion."

Tony Alessandra
- "The Platinum Rule: Do unto others as they want to be done on to. Treat people the way they want to be treated."

Tony Robbins
- "Surmounting difficulty is the crucible that forms character."

Warren Buffet
- "It takes 20 years to build a reputation and five minutes to ruin it. If you think about that, you'll do things differently."

Zig Ziglar
- "The foundation stones for a balanced success are honesty, character, integrity, faith, love and loyalty."

69

Be Couragous

Jerry's Tips:

- Courage is being afraid to do something and doing it anyway because you have decided it's more important to do it than to be afraid.

- Courage doesn't always roar. Sometimes it's just a quiet voice inside of you that says 'you can do it'.

Ambrose Redmoon
- "Courage is not the absence of fear, but rather the judgment that something else is more important than fear."

Anais Nin
- "Life shrinks or expands in proportion to one's courage."

Christopher Columbus
- "You can never cross the ocean unless you have the courage to lose sight of the shore."

Dale Carnegie
- "Most of us have far more courage than we ever dreamed we possessed."

Eddie Rickenbacker
- "Courage is doing what you're afraid to do. There can be no courage unless you're scared."

George Horace Lorimer
- "Because a fellow has failed once or twice, or a dozen times, you don't want to set him down as a failure till he's dead or loses his courage - and that's the same thing."

James Allen
"Whether you be man or woman you will never do anything in this world without courage. It is the greatest quality of the mind next to honor."

Mark Twain
"Courage is resistance to fear, mastery of fear -- not absence of fear."

Ralph Waldo Emerson
"Whatever course you decide upon, there is always someone to tell you that you are wrong. There are always difficulties arising which tempt you to believe that your critics are right. To map out a course of action and follow it to an end requires courage."

Reuben Gonzalez
"Success requires two types of courage: Courage to get started. Courage to not quit or give up."

Rollo May
"The opposite of courage in our society is not cowardice, it is conformity."

Thomas Edison
"Be courageous. I have seen many depressions in business. Always America has emerged from these stronger and more prosperous. Be brave as your fathers before you. Have faith! Go forward!"

Walt Disney
"All our dreams can come true, if we have the courage to pursue them."

Winston Churchill
"Courage is what it takes to stand up and speak, courage is also what it takes to sit down and listen."

70

Be Loving, Never Neglect Your Family

Jerry's Tips:

- Spend as much time with your spouse and children as possible. Enjoy every minute you spend with them and make them worthwhile for them and you.

- Hug your spouse and children every day and tell them you love them; you never know when it will be the last time. If you don't have a spouse or children then do this with your primary personal relationship.

Abraham Lincoln
- "It feels good to have money in your pocket, but it feels great to spend it on someone you love."

Ann Landers
- "If you have love in your life it can make up for a great many things you lack. If you don't have it, no matter what else there is, it's not enough."

Anonymous
- "Those who love deeply never grow old."

- "No matter what you've done for yourself or for humanity, if you can't look back on having given love and attention to your own family, what have you really accomplished?"

- "To be loved, you must be lovable."

Bruce Lee
- "Love is like a friendship caught on fire. In the beginning a flame, very pretty, often hot and fierce, but still only light and flickering. As love grows older, our hearts mature and our love becomes as coals, deep-burning and unquenchable."

David J. Schwartz
- "Do something special for your family often. It doesn't have to be something expensive. It's thoughtfulness that counts. Anything that shows that you put your family's interests first will do the trick."

- "Ask yourself each day what can I do to make my spouse and children happy?"

Henry Drummond
- "You will find as you look back upon your life that the moments when you have truly lived are the moments when you have done things in the spirit of love."

Jim Rohn
- "Your family and your love must be cultivated like a garden. Time, effort, and imagination must be summoned constantly to keep it flourishing and growing."

Leo Buscaglia
- "Love is life. And if you miss love, you miss life."

Mother Teresa
- "Smile at each other, smile at your wife, smile at your husband, smile at your children, smile at each other - it doesn't matter who it is - and that will help you to grow up in greater love for each other."

Nicholas Sparks
- "I think that enduring, committed love between a married couple, along with raising children, is the most noble act anyone can aspire to. It is not written about very much."

Sydney Smith
- "To love and to be loved is the greatest happiness of existence."

Victor Hugo
- "The supreme happiness in life is the conviction that we are loved."

71

Be Honest, Have Integrity, Always Keep Your Promises

Jerry's Tips:

- For people to trust you, your word must be impeccable. If you promise to do something you must do it.

- Once your word is broken you don't have much to say for yourself.

- Promise what you'll do, then do what you promise.

Alexander Hamilton
- "A promise must never be broken."

Anonymous
- "If you don't stand for something, you will fall for anything."

- "A good name, like good will, is attained by many actions and may be lost by one."

Benjamin Franklin
- "Honesty is the best policy."

Don Miguel Ruiz
- "Be Impeccable with your word. Speak with integrity. Say only what you mean. Avoid using the word to speak against yourself or to gossip about others. Use the power of your word in the direction of truth and love."

Donald Trump
- "It's not just business acumen but integrity that carries you forward in the business world. It's as simple as keeping your word or, in some cases, remembering what your words were."

- "Your personal reputation must be that you are responsible, professional and loyal."

- "I think one thing shines as gold. You need to deliver what you promise EVERY SINGLE TIME. That's the only way to get people to trust your brand and to believe in your product."

Dr. Laura Schlessinger
- "People with integrity do what they say they are going to do. Others have excuses."

Elvis Presley
- "Truth is like the sun. You can shut it out for a time, but it ain't goin' away."

General George S. Patton
- "Say what you mean and mean what you say."

H. Jackson Brown, Jr.
- "Live so that when your children think of fairness and integrity, they think of you."

Joe Paterno
- "Success without honor is an unseasoned dish; it will satisfy your hunger, but it won't taste good."

John Wooden
- "Never lie, never cheat, never steal."

Oprah Winfrey
- "Real integrity is doing the right thing, knowing that nobody's going to know whether you did it or not."

Pat Croce
- "Integrity has no on/off switch."

Thomas Jefferson
- "He who permits himself to tell a lie once, finds it easier to do it a second time."

PERSONAL CHARACTER COUNTS
BE HONEST, HAVE INTEGRITY, ALWAYS KEEP YOUR PROMISES

Thomas S. Monson
- "Perhaps the surest test of an individual's integrity is his refusal to do or say anything that would damage his self-respect."

W. Clement Stone
- "Have the courage to say no. Have the courage to face the truth. Do the right thing because it is right. These are the magic keys to living your life with integrity."

72

Be Happy And Lighten Up, Enjoy A Good Laugh

Jerry's Tips:

- Happiness is a choice. Why not be happy all the time? Being unhappy doesn't get you anywhere.

- Look at how young children laugh. They never pretend to laugh. When they are happy they laugh with all their soul and radiate happiness. That's how you should feel when you laugh.

Abraham Lincoln
- "Most people are about as happy as they make up their minds to be."

Albert Schweitzer
- "Success is not the key to happiness. Happiness is the key to success."

Anonymous
- "Enjoy life. There's plenty of time to be dead."

- "Cheerfulness removes the rust from the mind, lubricates our inward machinery, and enables us to do our work with fewer creaks and; groans. If people were universally cheerful, probably there wouldn't be half the quarreling or a tenth part of the wickedness; there is. Cheerfulness, too, promotes health and immortality. Cheerful people live longest here on earth, afterward in our hearts."

- "The happiest people don't necessarily have the best of everything... they make the best of everything..."

- "Happiness is a choice that requires effort at times."

Personal Character Counts
Be Happy and Lighten Up, Enjoy a Good Laugh

- "Happiness is the art of never holding in your mind the memory of any unpleasant thing that has passed."

Aristotle
- "Happiness is the meaning and the purpose of life, the whole aim and end of human existence."

Bill Cosby
- "You can turn painful situations around through laughter. If you can find humor in anything, even poverty, you can survive it."

Dale Carnegie
- "Are you bored with life? Then throw yourself into some work you believe in with all your heart, live for it, die for it, and you will find happiness that you had thought could never be yours."

- "Happiness doesn't depend on any external conditions, it is governed by our mental attitude."

Earl Nightingale
- "Learn to enjoy every minute of your life. Be happy now. Don't wait for something outside of yourself to make you happy in the future. Think how really precious is the time you have to spend, whether it's at work or with your family. Every minute should be enjoyed and savored."

- "Always keep that happy attitude. Pretend that you are holding a beautiful fragrant bouquet."

Groucho Marx
- "I, not events, have the power to make me happy or unhappy today. I can choose which it shall be. Yesterday is dead, tomorrow hasn't arrived yet. I have just one day, today, and I'm going to be happy in it."

Jim Rohn
- "Learn how to be happy with what you have while you pursue all that you want."

Leo Tolstoy
- "If you want to be happy, be."

Mark Twain

- "Humor is mankind's greatest blessing."

- "Humor is the great thing, the saving thing. The minute it crops up, all our irritations and resentments slip away and a sunny spirit takes their place."

- "Against the assault of laughter nothing can stand."

- "The best way to cheer yourself up is to try to cheer somebody else up."

Norman Vincent Peale

- "Who decides whether you shall be happy or unhappy? The answer — you do!"

- "Our happiness depends on the habit of mind we cultivate. So practice happy thinking every day. Cultivate the merry heart, develop the happiness habit, and life will become a continual feast."

Og Mandino

- "Laugh and your life will be lengthened for this is the great secret of long life."

- "Realize that true happiness lies within you. Waste no time and effort searching for peace and contentment and joy in the world outside. Remember that there is no happiness in having or in getting, but only in giving. Reach out. Share. Smile. Hug. Happiness is a perfume you cannot pour on others without getting a few drops on yourself."

Personal Character Counts
Be Happy and Lighten Up, Enjoy a Good Laugh

Red Skelton
- "I live by this credo: Have a little laugh at life and look around you for happiness instead of sadness. Laughter has always brought me out of unhappy situations. Even in your darkest moment, you usually can find something to laugh about if you try hard enough."

Robert R. Updegraff
- "Happiness is to be found along the way, not at the end of the road, for then the journey is over and it is too late. Today, this hour, this minute is the day, the hour, the minute for each of us to sense the fact that life is good, with all of its trials and troubles, and perhaps more interesting because of them."

Steven Covey
- "Happiness can be defined, in part at least, as the fruit of the desire and ability to sacrifice what we want now for what we want eventually."

W. Clement Stone
- "To be happy, make other people happy."

73

Be Charitable, Give Back, Be Generous

Jerry's Tips:

- Having all the riches in the world will not make you feel better than personally helping someone who is desperately struggling with a hardship. If you don't believe this try it sometime. It will change your life for the better.

Albert Einstein
- "It is every man's obligation to put back into the world at least the equivalent of what he takes out of it."

Eleanor Roosevelt
- "Since you get more joy out of giving joy to others, you should put a good deal of thought into the happiness that you are able to give."

Jim Rohn
- "One person caring about another represents life's greatest value."

John D. Rockefeller, Jr.
- "Think of giving not as a duty but as a privilege."

John Wooden
- "You can't live a perfect day without doing something for someone who will never be able to repay you."

Oprah Winfrey
- "I don't think you ever stop giving. I really don't. I think it's an on-going process. And it's not just about being able to write a check. It's being able to touch somebody's life."

Tony Robbins
- "Life is a gift, and it offers us the privilege, opportunity, and responsibility to give something back by becoming more."

PERSONAL CHARACTER COUNTS
BE CHARITABLE, GIVE BACK, BE GENEROUS

- "Only those who have learned the power of sincere and selfless contribution experience life's deepest joy: true fulfillment."

Winston Churchill
- "We make a living by what we get, but we make a life by what we give."

74

Be Kind

Jerry's Tips:

- Your words of kindness cost you nothing and are worth so much to those who receive them.

- Never mistake being kind with being a push over. The former is a virtue the later is a weakness.

Aesop
- "No act of kindness, no matter how small, is ever wasted."

Blaise Pascal
- "Kind words do not cost much. Yet they accomplish much."

Dalai Lama
- "My religion is very simple. My religion is kindness."

Kahlil Gibran
- "Tenderness and kindness are not signs of weakness and despair, but manifestations of strength and resolutions."

Louis Nizer
- "Words of comfort, skillfully administered, are the oldest therapy known to man."

Mother Teresa
- "Be kind and merciful. Let no one ever come to you without coming away better and happier."

PERSONAL CHARACTER COUNTS
BE KIND

Napoleon Hill
- "Until you have learned to be tolerant with those who do not always agree with you; until you have cultivated the habit of saying some kind word of those whom you do not admire; until you have formed the habit of looking for the good instead of the bad there is in others, you will be neither successful nor happy."

Og Mandino
- "Beginning today, treat everyone you meet as if they were going to be dead by midnight. Extend to them all the care, kindness and understanding you can muster, and do it with no thought of any reward. Your life will never be the same again."

Ralph Waldo Emerson
- "You cannot do a kindness too soon, for you never know when it will be too late."

William Penn
- "I expect to pass through this life but once. If, therefore there can be any kindness I can show or any good thing I can do for any fellow being let me do it now, and not defer or neglect it, as I shall not pass this way again."

75

Be Respectful

Jerry's Tips:

- When you respect other people you respect yourself.

- The poorest and weakest people need our respect the most.

Albert Einstein
- "Everyone should be respected as an individual, but no one idolized."

Buddha
- "You should respect each other and refrain from disputes; you should not, like water and oil, repel each other, but should, like milk and water, mingle together."

Frank Barron
- "Never take a person's dignity: it is worth everything to them, and nothing to you."

H. Jackson Brown, Jr.
- "Never deprive someone of hope; it might be all they have."

Ralph Waldo Emerson
- "Every human being, of whatever origin, of whatever station, deserves respect. We must each respect others even as we respect ourselves."

Dr. Robert H. Schuller
- "As we grow as unique persons, we learn to respect the uniqueness of others."

76

Be Grateful

Jerry's Tips:

- You demonstrate gratitude when you are thankful and appreciative for something in your life.

- When you wake up each day be grateful for your life.

- Don't hesitate to thank and compliment people.

Buddha
- "Let us rise up and be thankful, for if we didn't learn a lot today, at least we learned a little, and if we didn't learn a little, at least we didn't get sick, and if we got sick, at least we didn't die; so, let us all be thankful."

Cicero
- "Gratitude is not only the greatest of virtues, but the parent of all the others."

Meister Eckhart
- "If the only prayer you said in your whole life was, 'thank you,' that would suffice."

Melody Beattie
- "Gratitude unlocks the fullness of life. It turns what we have into enough, and more. It turns denial into acceptance, chaos into order, confusion into clarity.... It turns problems into gifts, failures into success, the unexpected into perfect timing, and mistakes into important events. Gratitude makes sense of our past, brings peace for today and creates a vision for tomorrow."

77

Be Humble

Jerry's Tips:

- If you do something great, people will find out. Don't cheapen your accomplishment by bragging or boasting about it.

- Just because you are humble doesn't mean you can't politely tell people that you are a winner and very good at what you do.

- Being humble does not mean you need to be a sheep.

- Many of the strongest, hard hitting and fierce athletes are very humble people when they are outside of where they compete, and do not brag about themselves or their accomplishments.

Aesop
- "The smaller the mind the greater the conceit."

Benjamin Franklin
- "A man wrapped up in himself makes a very small bundle."

Blaise Pascal
- "Do you wish people to think well of you? Don't speak well of yourself."

John Wooden
- "Talent is God given. Be humble. Fame is man-given. Be grateful. Conceit is self-given. Be careful."

Johnny Unitis
- "There is a difference between conceit and confidence. Conceit is bragging about yourself. Confidence means you believe you can get the job done."

78

Be Forgiving

Jerry's Tips:

- When you forgive anyone including yourself you are saying I know you did something wrong but I believe you can change and improve and not do the same thing again.

- When you forgive someone you free yourself from having to carry around your negative emotion towards them.

- It's good to forgive; but don't ever forget what they did and why they did it.

- When you forgive someone you do not change the past but you do enlarge your future with him or her.

Alden Nowlan
- "The day the child realizes that all adults are imperfect, he becomes an adolescent; the day he forgives them, he becomes an adult; the day he forgives himself, he becomes wise."

Alexander Pope
- "To err is human; to forgive, divine."

Anonymous
- "It takes a strong person to say sorry, and an ever stronger person to forgive."

Catherine Ponder
- "When you hold resentment toward another, you are bound to that person or condition by an emotional link that is stronger than steel. Forgiveness is the only way to dissolve that link and get free."

THE SUCCESS FORMULA FOR PERSONAL GROWTH

Confucius
- "The more you know yourself, the more you forgive yourself."

Desmond Tutu
- "Without forgiveness, there's no future."

Mohandas Gandhi
- "If we practice an eye for an eye and a tooth for a tooth, soon the whole world will be blind and toothless."

- "The weak can never forgive. Forgiveness is the attribute of the strong."

John F. Kennedy
- "Forgive your enemies, but never forget their names."

Joshua L. Liebman
- "We achieve inner health only through forgiveness - the forgiveness not only of others but also of ourselves."

Josh McDowell
- "Forgiveness is the oil of relationships."

Les Brown
- "Forgive yourself for your faults and your mistakes and move on."

- "Forgive those who have hurt you."

Lewis B. Smedes
- "To forgive is to set a prisoner free and discover that the prisoner was you."

Martin Luther King, Jr.
- "We must develop and maintain the capacity to forgive. He who is devoid of the power to forgive is devoid of the power to love. There is some good in the worst of us and some evil in the best of us. When we discover this, we are less prone to hate our enemies."

Oscar Wilde
- "Always forgive your enemies - nothing annoys them so much."

Personal Character Counts
Be Forgiving

Thomas Fuller
- "He that cannot forgive others breaks the bridge over which he must pass himself; for every man has need to be forgiven."

Thomas S. Szasz
- "The stupid neither forgive nor forget; the naive forgive and forget; the wise forgive but do not forget."

79

Don't Envy Or Be Jealous

Jerry's Tips:

- You poison your own ambition by being envious of other people's accomplishments or possessions. Instead of envying them, consider it proof that, with hard work, you too can obtain what they have.

- Never envy someone; it elevates them in your mind to being superior to you. You should always believe that you are just as good as anyone else, and that with hard work you can be the best you can be.

Alexander Solzhenitsyn
- "Our envy of others devours us most of all."

Antisthenes
- "As iron is eaten by rust, so are the envious consumed by envy."

Brian Tracy
- "If you envy successful people, you create a negative force field of attraction that repels you from ever doing the things that you need to do to be successful. If you admire successful people, you create a positive force field of attraction that draws you toward becoming more and more like the kinds of people that you want to be like."

Buddha
- "Do not overrate what you have received, nor envy others. He who envies others does not obtain peace of mind."

Honore de Balzac
- "Envy is the most stupid of vices, for there is no single advantage to be gained from it."

Samuel Johnson
- "Whoever envies another confesses his superiority."

80

Release Your Anger

Jerry's Tips:

- Unfulfilled expectations produce anger, and if not released, anger will turn to bitterness. Bitterness leads to resentment, which leads to revenge, that leads to not being grateful, which leads to hopelessness and despair.

- Anger is a fire that burns inside of you, that if it is not extinguished will consume everything good about you.

- Being angry at someone does no one any good. You must release your anger and take action to deal with the underlying cause.

Anonymous
- "For every minute you are angry, you lose sixty seconds of happiness."

Chuck Norris
- "Men are like steel. When they lose their temper, they lose their worth."

General Colin Powell
- "Get mad, Then get over it."

Mark Twain
- "Anger is an acid that can do more harm to the vessel in which it is stored than to anything on which it is poured."

Sidney J. Harris
- "If a small thing has the power to make you angry, does that not indicate something about your size?"

THE SUCCESS FORMULA FOR PERSONAL GROWTH

Thomas Jefferson
- "When angry count to ten before you speak. If very angry, count to one hundred."

81

Exercise

Sound Mind In A Sound Body

Jerry's Tips:

- If you have a strong body to carry around your strong mind, and take strong action, you will be more successful than someone who is physically very weak and always tired.

- When you exercise your body your mind gets a better house to live in.

- Exercising today is a long term investment in your health.

- To be successful you need a flexible, strong and quick mind and a flexible, strong and quick body.

- There is an inseparable connection between your mind and body. If one of them is weak the other cannot reach its full potential.

Bobby Fischer
- "Your body has to be in top condition. Your chess deteriorates as your body does. You can't separate body from mind."

Jack Lalanne
- "Do you know how many calories are in butter and cheese and ice cream? Would you get your dog up in the morning for a cup of coffee and a donut?"

THE SUCCESS FORMULA FOR PERSONAL GROWTH

Pat Croce
- "I am all about work hard, play hard. But I also support the concept of rest hard. I believe it's vital that your mind and body recover and recuperate from the stresses and strains of the day and/or week. Recharge your batteries. Read a good book. Veg out on an engaging movie or television show. Get lost in a passionate hobby. Play with the kids. But do it as I do and dress to rest. That's right! I'm not talking about dress to impress. It's just the opposite – it's chillin' time. You can shed that red power tie or those fancy high heels, or you can keep them on…whatever works for you. Lounge clothing can run the gamut as far as I'm concerned. There are no rules…under the condition you really dress to rest and switch off the left side of your brain."

Ralph Waldo Emerson
- "The first wealth is health."

Tony Robbins
- "The higher your energy level, the more efficient your body. The more efficient your body, the better you feel and the more you will use your talent to produce outstanding results."

82

Money Isn't Everything, But It's Right Up There With Oxygen

Jerry's Tips:

- I'm a spiritual person as well as a realist. The fact is, that unless you live in a cave you need money to live, and the more money you have the better you can provide for yourself and your family.

- No matter how much money you want to earn, you must learn how to earn, save and invest, or else you won't have much when you need it.

- Live below your means.

- Limit your personal debt as much as possible and use it to purchase assets, not merely things you consume, wear or use up.

- Save 10% of what you earn and invest it in low risk investments so it will grow and provide you income when you are old.

- Only take investment advice from someone who is an expert.

Benjamin Franklin
- "A penny saved is a penny earned."

David J. Schwartz
- "It's just as much fun to 'spend' money on savings as it is to spend it on something else."

Dr. Joyce Brothers
- "The world at large does not judge us by who we are and what we know; it judges us by what we have."

George S. Clason
- "It is true that money cannot buy happiness but it does make it possible for you to enjoy the best that the world has to offer."

George Bernard Shaw
- "Lack of money is the root of all evil."

Jim Rohn
- "Profits are better than wages."

Ogden Nash
- "If you don't want to work you have to work to earn enough money so that you won't have to work."

Oprah Winfrey
- "What material success does is provide you with the ability to concentrate on other things that really matter. And that is being able to make a difference, not only in your own life, but in other people's lives."

Orison Swett Marden
- "The man who has no money is poor, but one who has nothing but money is poorer. He only is rich who can enjoy without owning; he is poor who though he has millions is covetous."

Pat Croce
- "The safest way to double your money is to fold it in half and put it back in your pocket! I can hear my dad to this day, saying: don't spend it, save it!"

- "I do believe the basics of a personal financial plan should be to spend less than you gain and invest the difference and should include at least four personal financial statements within easy reach of your fingertips.

  The four personal financial statements that I regularly update and peruse are: a net worth statement, a budget, a financial vision statement, and a credit report. All four tools can help you adhere to the number-one secret of gaining wealth: spend less than you earn and invest the difference."

MONEY ISN'T EVERYTHING
BUT IT'S RIGHT UP THERE WITH OXYGEN

- "A budget provides you with the power to take control of your choices and decide if the money is being spent the best way possible. For example, during my annual family budget review I was disgusted with the monthly amount – specifically within the housing account - I was paying for our cable TV expense. It seemed an outrageous waste of money. So by eliminating all of the premium channels except HBO, we saved $56 monthly, resulting in a savings of $672 yearly. And even though this may not seem like a lot of money, it's the little changes that make the big difference. As Ben Franklin said so pragmatically, 'A small leak can sink a great ship.' And I not only want to stay afloat, I want to cruise on to my destiny."

Robert G. Allen

- "Money is one of the most important subjects of your entire life. Some of life's greatest enjoyments and most of life's greatest disappointments stem from your decisions about money. Whether you experience great peace of mind or constant anxiety will depend on getting your finances under control."

Robert Kiyosaki

- "The main reason people struggle financially is because they have spent years in school but learned nothing about money. The result is that people learn to work for money...but never to have money work for them."

- "Don't say 'I can't afford it,' and instead ask 'HOW can I afford it?'"

- "If you want to be successful ... when it comes to money, you have got to know the difference between facts and opinions. You must know numbers. You must know the facts."

- "If you do not know how to care for money, money will stay away from you."

- "Many of today's youth have credit cards before they leave high school, yet they have never had a course in money or how to invest it, let alone understand how compound interest works on credit cards."

- "The poor and middle class work for money. The rich have money work for them."

THE SUCCESS FORMULA FOR PERSONAL GROWTH

Suze Orman

- "There's nothing wrong with saying, 'I want to have more,' 'I want to be more,' 'I did this for money.' "

- "One has to understand that money has to play a vital role in your life. It's not a dirty role or a role that you should be ashamed of. It's not a role that should be a disgrace at all."

- "Although money alone won't make us happy, the lack of money surely will make us miserable."

Warren Buffet

- "Rule No.1: Never lose money.
    Rule No.2: Never forget rule No.1."

Will Smith

- "Too many people spend money they haven't earned, to buy things they don't want, to impress people they don't like."

Zig Ziglar

- "Money isn't the most important thing in life, but it's reasonably close to oxygen on the 'gotta have it' scale."

- "Almost without exception, you can measure a person's contribution to society in terms of dollars. The more he contributes, the more he earns."

83

How To Increase Your Luck

Jerry's Tips:

- Luck is the Universe taking deliberate action as part of its plan to achieve its goal for you!

- There's no magic to becoming lucky. If you want to be lucky, develop expertise in something and look for ways to apply it.

- Most good luck is the result of a person's hard work and good judgment making choices in their life. Most bad luck is the result of the lack of these actions.

- Bad luck happens to people who are lazy, have a negative attitude, don't have any valuable skills, don't learn from their mistakes, don't get along well with other people, and don't set goals or don't take sufficient action to achieve their goals – Do you want to guess how to have good luck?

- No one but you truly knows the great effort you have put in to achieve what others think was obtained through pure luck. Even buying a lottery ticket every week for years before you win takes effort.

- People confuse luck with chance. Chance is gambling at a casino where you have no control over the outcome. Luck is about probabilities, and you do have control over your outcomes in life, because you can increase your ability to be prepared and ready to take advantage of an opportunity that comes your way.

Anonymous
- "Luck is a crossroad where preparation and opportunity meet."

THE SUCCESS FORMULA FOR PERSONAL GROWTH

Anne Tyler
- "People always call it luck when you've acted more sensibly than they have."

Bruce Springsteen
- "When it comes to luck, you make your own."

Cybil Franklin
- "It's amazing how lucky I become whenever I consistently put out my best effort."

Gary Player
- "The harder I work, the luckier I get."

Harry Golden
- "The only thing that overcomes hard luck is hard work."

Lucille Ball
- "Luck? I don't know anything about luck. I've never banked on it, and I'm afraid of people who do. Luck to me is something else: Hard work -- and realizing what is opportunity and what isn't."

Michael Korda
- "Luck can often mean simply taking advantage of a situation at the right moment. It is possible to make your luck by being always prepared."

Og Mandino
- "Lucky is what others will call you after your hard work produces results."

Oprah Winfrey
- "I feel that luck is preparation meeting opportunity."

Ralph Waldo Emerson
- "Good luck is another name for tenacity of purpose."

Ray Kroc
- "Luck is a dividend of sweat. The more you sweat, the luckier you get."

Thomas Jefferson
- "I'm a great believer in luck and I find the harder I work, the more I have of it."

84

The Power Of Personal Momentum

Jerry's Tips:

- Don't worry how hard it is to start working toward a personal goal. Starting anything that will pay off for you will always require hard work. Keep in mind that once you get it going you don't have to work as hard to keep it going.

- The greatest effort is to go from nothing to something. Once you decide on a goal, figure out how to achieve it, and start taking massive action to accomplish it, your peddling on the road to success will get much easier.

- Never work with so little effort that you accomplish nothing, or work too hard that you burn out. For long lasting success, learn what your optimum momentum is and try to maintain it in everything you do.

- Working at a constant momentum keeps your motivation up and your productivity high.

Aesop
- "Slow and steady wins the race."

Charles J. Givens
- "Success requires first expending ten units of effort to produce one unit of results. Your momentum will then produce ten units of results with each unit of effort."

Donald Trump
- "Momentum is something you have to work at to maintain. Find your own current and then go with it! Don't allow for distractions. Do everything you can to maintain your energy flow. Watch out for streaks of momentum that you can't sustain — keep your equilibrium in all things, even in your energy output."

THE SUCCESS FORMULA FOR PERSONAL GROWTH

Michael Korda
- "One way to keep momentum going is to have constantly greater goals."

Oprah Winfrey
- "If you neglect to recharge a battery, it dies. And if you run full speed ahead without stopping for water, you lose momentum to finish the race."

William Osler
- "To create momentum in your life Never leave the scene of a decision without taking action. The action has to be:
  1. in support of your decision no matter how insignificant the action might seem, and
  2. the action has to be something your willing to do right now."

85

Want More Out Of Life?
Be A Little Restless And Discontented

Jerry's Tips:

- Always be grateful for what you have now, and where you are at in your life, because no matter what you currently have many people are far worse off than you; But also remember, that feeling a little restless and discontented to be better than you are today, will spur you on to make you improve.

- Whether you are presently successful or not, if you get too comfortable with your life you will stagnate and deteriorate.

- Complacency leads to poor performance and poor results because its friends are smugness, apathy and inaction, and its enemies are concern, desire and taking decisive determined action to accomplish your goals.

Anonymous
- "Discontent is the seed of growth."

Carl Sandburg
- "Before you go to sleep, say to yourself, 'I haven't reached my goal yet, whatever it is, and I'm going to be uncomfortable and in a degree unhappy until I do.' When you do reach it, find another."

David Rockefeller
- "If necessity is the mother of invention, discontent is the father of progress."

Ella Wheeler Wilcox
- "The splendid discontent of God with Chaos made the world... And from the discontent of man the world's best progress springs."

Eugene Victor Debs
- "If it had not been for the discontent of a few fellows who had not been satisfied with their conditions, you would still be living in caves. Intelligent discontent is the mainspring of civilization. Progress is born of agitation. It is agitation or stagnation."

Louis L'Amour
- "Nobody got anywhere in the world by simply being content."

Og Mandino
- "Do not allow yesterday's success to lull you into today's complacency, for this is the great foundation of failure."

Oscar Wilde
- "Discontent is the first step in the progress of a man or a nation."

Thomas Edison
- "Restlessness is discontent and discontent is the first necessity of progress. Show me a thoroughly satisfied man and I will show you a failure."

- "We shall have no better conditions in the future if we are satisfied with all those which we have at present."

Tony Robbins
- "You must learn how to handle complacency. Comfort can be one of the most disastrous emotions a body could have."

86

Ask Lots Of Questions

Jerry's Tips:

- It sounds simple but the truth is, successful people ask themselves, and other success oriented people, lots of questions about how to succeed in life, which gives them answers and knowledge, which allows them to construct a good plan for their personal growth and success - unsuccessful people don't ask these types of questions.

- If you don't ask a question about something you don't presently know, it's likely you will never know the answer.

- When you ask a question you focus thought on a choice or problem.

- If you ask a question you will get an answer. The answer may or not be something you like, but you will get an answer and you can then devise a plan and take action to get you where you need to go.

- Look at very young children, they ask questions all day long, it's programmed into their DNA to ask questions so they can learn and develop.

- If you want to be successful start asking yourself lots of questions such as: 'What skill do I have or want to develop, that I enjoy doing and can provide value to people or solve their problems, that I can earn a good living doing?'

- A successful Entrepreneur asks: 'What can I do differently from my competitors to provide extra value to my customers?' In the same way, an employee or student can adopt this mindset and figure out how to stand out to get ahead.

THE SUCCESS FORMULA FOR PERSONAL GROWTH

- At the end of the day, ask yourself questions about what you did that day, such as: 'What did I do today that I am proud of? What did I do today that I didn't do well and need to improve?' Asking questions like these force you to see where your life is going, and they help you to stay motivated while working on your goals, and to make corrections when needed.

- If you have a question never be embarrassed or afraid to ask it.

Albert Einstein
- "The important thing is to not stop questioning."

Anonymous
- "The only stupid question is the one you don't ask."

Benjamin Disraeli
- "The fool wonders, the wise man asks."

Bruce Lee
- "A wise man can learn more from a foolish question than a fool can learn from a wise answer."

Chinese Proverb
- "He who asks a question is a fool for five minutes. He who does not ask a question remains a fool forever."

James Allen
- "For true success ask yourself these four questions: Why? Why not? Why not me? Why not now?"

Jim Rohn
- "Where are my thoughts taking me?"

Og Mandino
- "Take the attitude of a student, never be too big to ask questions, never know too much to learn something new."

Pat Croce
- "I know that I don't know what I don't know, so I continually listen, question, and observe."

Ask Lots of Questions

Pablo Picasso
- "Others have seen what is and asked why. I have seen what could be and asked why not."

Tony Robbins
- "Successful people ask better questions, and as a result, they get better answers."

- "How am I going to live today in order to create the tomorrow I'm committed to?"

- "The most powerful way to change your focus is through the use of questions."

- "In what direction are you presently going? If you follow your current direction, where will you be in five years or ten years? And is that where you want to go? If not, you can and you should change."

Voltaire
- "Judge a man by his questions, not by his answers."

W. Edwards Deming
- "If you do not know how to ask the right question, you discover nothing."

W. Clement Stone
- "If there is something to gain and nothing to lose by asking, by all means ask!"

About The Author

Jerry Bruckner is an American author, publisher, husband and proud father of his energetic and creative 3-three-year-old girl, Brianna Bruckner.

Jerry was born and raised in New York City. He is committed to personal growth and mentoring others to help them grow, develop and succeed.

Jerry studied various martial arts for 25 years and was the Captain of his College's Karate team. He also was a member of his College's competitive swim team, and was a co-winner of the College's grueling 500 mile swim, bike and run competition, which raised money for charity. Jerry has served as an American Red Cross Certified Life Guard Instructor, and has taught swimming to many people from age 2 to 70.

After a much less than stellar start, Jerry graduated with Honors from College, attended and graduated from New York Law School, and practiced Law for 10 years in the New York State and Federal Courts, focusing on cases that helped people, including free pro bono cases to help low income people create Wills and handle their other family issues.

A lover of all types of music, Jerry plays guitar and also started a company that provided live concert sound systems to rock bands.

Jerry admits to having a geek side and loves technology. He taught himself computer programming, initially as a hobby, and went on to work on very large and complex software development projects, for one of the largest software companies in the world. He has also managed software development projects that collaborated across multiple countries.

One of Jerry's personal convictions that describes his attitude toward personal development is: "You only get one chance to play the game of life… be thankful for every day and whatever you have… give it all you got… with whatever you've got… to do your best to reach your maximum potential to provide for yourself and your family, and to give back to the Community!"

Jerry loves to hear from his readers. To contact Jerry or send feedback about this book, please send an email to: SuccessFormulaForPersonalGrowth@yahoo.com

Index

Abigail Van Buren, 274

Abraham Lincoln, 36, 75, 86, 142, 155, 224, 230, 274, 279, 284

Abraham Maslow, 180

Adlai E. Stevenson, 155, 188

Aesop, 290, 294, 309

Al Duncan, 64

Albert Einstein, 33, 125, 156, 180, 214, 265, 268, 274, 288, 292, 314

Albert Schweitzer, 284

Alden Nowlan, 295

Aldous Huxley, 173

Alexander Graham Bell, 75, 82, 86, 265

Alexander Hamilton, 281

Alexander Pope, 295

Alexander Solzhenitsyn, 298

Alfred A. Montapert, 47, 94

Alice Foote Macdougall, 237

Althea Gibson, 75

Ambrose Redmoon, 277

Amelia Earhart, 36

Anais Nin, 277

Andre Gide, 209

Andrew Carnegie, 111, 128, 167, 246

Andy and Larry Wachowski, 192

Andy Munthe, 156

Ann Landers, 224, 279

Anna Jameson, 68

Anna Pavlova, 135

Anne Tyler, 308

Anonymous, 22, 36, 43, 65, 68, 86, 90, 97, 109, 111, 115, 119, 134, 142, 150, 156, 167, 188, 193, 205, 210, 233, 234, 237, 241, 246, 255, 261, 268, 274, 279, 281, 284, 295, 299, 307, 311, 314

Antisthenes, 298

Arie de Geus, 75

Aristotle, 47, 51, 65, 98, 197, 230, 285

Aristotle Onassis, 177, 230

Armstrong Williams, 234

Arnold H. Glasow, 16, 98, 246

Arnold Palmer, 82, 128, 156

Art Turock, 109

Arthur Ashe, 17, 87

Ashley Tisdale, 203

Ayn Rand, 265

Babatunde Olatunji, 262

Babe Ruth, 156, 197, 242, 262

Baltasar Gracian, 142

Barack Obama, 180

Belva Davis, 214

Ben Stein, 98

Benjamin Disraeli, 3, 36, 55, 68, 75, 87, 156, 180, 314

Benjamin Ewise, 98

Benjamin Fairless, 181

Benjamin Franklin, 36, 43, 44, 51, 75, 87, 119, 156, 205, 224, 230, 237, 255, 265, 281, 294, 303

Bernice Johnson Reagon, 181

Bill Bradley, 246

Bill Clinton, 150

Bill Cosby, 156, 198, 262, 285

Bill Gates, 181, 255

Billie Jean King, 37, 80

Bjorn Borg, 157

Blaise Pascal, 17, 55, 212, 290, 294

Bo Bennett, 203, 230, 255

Bo Jackson, 98

Bob Boshnack, 150, 215

Bob Burg, 235

Bob Cousy, 128

Bob Dylan, 17

Bob Moawad, 37

Bob Proctor, 60, 75, 94, 98, 142

Bobby Fischer, 87, 301

Bobby Knight, 87

Booker T. Washington, 128

Brian Tracy, 2, 17, 22, 27, 37, 52, 69, 75, 94, 111, 142, 157, 186, 188, 210, 242, 255, 298

Bruce Barton, 142

Bruce Lee, 30, 55, 60, 76, 80, 82, 87, 91, 98, 115, 119, 135, 188, 205, 224, 280, 314

Bruce Springsteen, 308

Buddha, 27, 55, 262, 292, 293, 298

C. Northcote Parkinson, 256

C.S. Lewis, 29

Calvin Coolidge, 157

Carl Bard, 27

Carl Jung, 173

Carl Sandburg, 311

Carlos Castaneda, 174

Carol Burnett, 37

Catherine Ponder, 295

Catherine Pulsifer, 43, 47, 99, 116, 119, 188, 210

Cavett Robert, 142, 230

Cecil B. De Mille, 17

Charles (Tremendous) Jones, 98

Charles A. Garfield, 215

Charles C. Noble, 99

Charles Darwin, 189, 256

Charles Dickens, 91

Charles F. Kettering, 60, 177

Charles Gow, 135

Charles J. Givens, 309

Charles Lindbergh, 137

Charles R. Swindoll, 150, 265

Charles Schwab, 131, 246
Cherokee Indian Story, 275
Cherokee Proverb, 262
Chinese Proverb, 174, 314
Chin-Ning Chu, 198
Chris Evert, 65
Christopher Columbus, 277
Christopher Morley, 17
Christopher Reeve, 37
Chuck Norris, 157, 198, 299
Cicero, 293
Clint Eastwood, 150
Confucius, 2, 37, 65, 81, 87, 116, 157, 181, 275, 296
Conrad Hilton, 157
Cybil Franklin, 308
Dalai Lama, 290
Dale Carnegie, 25, 52, 65, 91, 131, 137, 157, 168, 181, 198, 225, 230, 242, 277, 285
Dan Kennedy, 256
David Blaine, 60
David J. Schwartz, 27, 43, 44, 47, 55, 60, 76, 99, 116, 119, 132, 143, 150, 171, 181, 193, 198, 206, 215, 219, 237, 242, 269, 272, 280, 303
David Rockefeller, 311
David Sarnoff, 157
David Viscott, 37
Dean Rusk, 231
Dee Hock, 272
Deepak Chopra, 17, 47

Demosthenes, 265
Denis Waitley, 38, 99, 111, 177, 193, 262
Derek Bok, 76
Desmond Tutu, 296
Don Miguel Ruiz, 281
Donald Trump, 55, 65, 76, 91, 94, 116, 120, 158, 174, 177, 181, 199, 233, 262, 281, 309
Douglas Lurtan, 94
Dr. Joyce Brothers, 144, 174, 303
Dr. Laura Schlessinger, 282
Dr. Maxwell Maltz, 25, 102, 136, 137, 145, 181, 201, 216, 266
Dr. Phil, 72, 174
Dr. Robert H. Schuller, 58, 144, 164, 266, 292
Dr. Spencer Johnston, 189
Dr. W. Edwards Deming, 126
Duke of Wellington, 76
Dwight D. Eisenhower, 151, 247
Earl Nightingale, 17, 38, 43, 55, 65, 99, 111, 132, 138, 151, 199, 216, 219, 242, 269, 270, 285
Eckhart Tolle, 262
Ed Parker, 206
Eddie Rickenbacker, 151, 277
Eddie Robinson, 158
Edwin Land, 272
Elbert Hubbard, 18, 87, 100, 193
Eleanor Roosevelt, 199, 288

Elizabeth Kubler-Ross, 47
Ella Wheeler Wilcox, 311
Elvis Presley, 282
Emile Coue, 219
English Proverb, 158
Epictetus, 30, 269
Eric Hoffer, 189
Ernest Hemingway, 225
Etienne de Grellet, 256
Eugene Victor Debs, 312
Euripides, 2
Florence Nightingale, 43
Francis Bacon, 78, 135, 256
Francois de La Rochefoucauld, 225
Frank Barron, 292
Frank Bettger, 231
Frank Herbert, 200
Frank Marino, 158
Frank Tibolt, 120
Frank Tyger, 265
Franklin D. Roosevelt, 151, 159, 193
Frederick Douglass, 159
Fyodor Dostoyevsky, 144
Gale Sayers, 159
Gary Player, 308
Gene Roddenberry, 38
General Colin Powell, 52, 87, 120, 151, 299
General Douglas MacArthur, 247
General George S. Patton, 43, 120, 128, 135, 138, 159, 200, 248, 282
General Norman Schwarzkopf, 186
George Bernard Shaw, 45, 135, 189, 212, 304
George Burns, 65
George Eliot, 27
George Horace Lorimer, 277
George Lucas, 61, 66, 159, 193
George Matthew Adams, 27, 56
George S. Clason, 304
George Washington Carver, 44
Georges Bernanos, 120
Giovanni Niccolini, 68, 111
Gloria Estefan, 265
Gloria Steinem, 269
Greg Anderson, 100
Greg Norman, 18
Groucho Marx, 285
H. Jackson Brown, Jr., 25, 159, 256, 282, 292
H. L. Hunt, 174
Hank Aaron, 159
Hannibal, 159
Harold Taylor, 69
Harriet Beecher Stowe, 160
Harry Browne, 135
Harry Golden, 308
Harry S. Truman, 151
Harvey Fierstein, 233
Helen Keller, 69, 144, 151, 160

Henri-Frederic Amiel, 174
Henrik Ibsen, 225
Henry David Thoreau, 25, 69, 100, 144
Henry Drummond, 280
Henry Ford, 27, 56, 77, 100, 144, 160, 169, 177, 182, 200, 225, 243, 256
Henry J. Heinz, 272
Henry Kravis, 275
Henry Van Dyke, 91
Henry Wadsworth Longfellow, 160, 262
Heraclitus, 189
Honore de Balzac, 298
Horace, 182
Horace Mann, 52
Howard Schultz, 248
Irvine Robbins, 272
Isaac Asimov, 189
Isaac Newton, 2, 160
J. C. Penney, 100
J. K. Rowling, 47, 61
J. Michael Straczynski, 44
J. P. Morgan, 112
J. Paul Getty, 272
Jack Canfield, 38, 66, 94
Jack Dempsey, 160
Jack Lalanne, 301
Jack Nicklaus, 193
Jack Welch, 38, 77, 91, 182, 189, 248
Jackie Collins, 120
Jackie Robinson, 30, 38
Jacob A. Riis, 160
James Allen, 45, 47, 56, 61, 69, 72, 94, 138, 160, 200, 278, 314
James J. Corbett, 160
James W. Newman, 144
Japanese Proverb, 121, 151
Jay Leno, 169
Jean Louis Etienne, 171
Jean Nidetch, 47
Jeff Bezos, 237
Jeff Keller, 200
Jeffrey Immelt, 248
Jerry West, 161
Jesse Owens, 161
Jesus Christ, 57, 275
Jiddu Krishnamurti, 200
Jim Carrey, 266
Jim Collins, 48, 66, 69, 77, 128, 161
Jim Rohn, 18, 25, 29, 30, 33, 38, 47, 52, 61, 66, 73, 77, 81, 100, 121, 128, 135, 161, 168, 175, 206, 225, 237, 242, 249, 256, 266, 269, 272, 280, 285, 288, 304, 314
Jinger Heath, 266
Joan Baez, 48
Joan Collins, 182
Joe Dimaggio, 121
Joe Montana, 112
Joe Namath, 87
Joe Paterno, 88, 112, 282

Johann Wolfgang von Goethe, 262

John C. Maxwell, 48, 57, 94, 121, 226

John D. Rockefeller, Jr., 161, 288

John Dewey, 88

John Donne, 243

John Dryden, 52

John F. Kennedy, 189, 296

John Hancock, 231

John Keats, 182

John McEnroe, 144, 161, 182

John Quincy Adams, 161, 249

John Sculley, 182, 266

John Wanamaker, 121

John Wayne, 200

John Wooden, 18, 25, 45, 88, 91, 128, 186, 263, 275, 282, 288, 294

Johnny Carson, 66

Johnny Unitis, 294

Jose Ortega y Gasset, 83

Joseph Heller, 138

Josh McDowell, 296

Joshua L. Liebman, 296

Judith M. Bardwick, 145

Julius Irving, 101

Kahlil Gibran, 290

Kareem Abdul Jabbar, 186

Kenneth Cole, 145

Kiana Tom, 101

Kurt Lewin, 101

Kurt Thomas, 101

Lance Armstrong, 61

Lao Tzu, 39, 81, 121, 177, 182, 193

Larry Bird, 128

Larry Ellison, 273

Laurence J. Peter, 231

Learned Hand, 175

Lee Iacocca, 107, 121, 161, 189, 226, 257, 266

Leo Burnett, 69

Leo Buscaglia, 280

Leo Tolstoy, 285

Leonardo da Vinci, 31, 77, 121, 190

Les Brown, 18, 22, 33, 39, 73, 77, 91, 101, 121, 128, 145, 161, 168, 171, 182, 194, 200, 226, 231, 269, 275, 296

Lewis B. Smedes, 296

Lou Holtz, 151

Louis D. Brandeis, 135

Louis E. Boone, 39

Louis L'Amour, 312

Louis Nizer, 290

Louis Pasteur, 162

Louisa May Alcott, 257

Lucille Ball, 308

Lyndon B. Johnson, 231

M. Scott Peck, 81

Madonna, 39

Mae West, 227

Magic Johnson, 243

Malcolm S. Forbes, 66, 91, 182

Marcus Aurelius, 57, 69, 194, 203, 257

Marcus Garvey, 145

Margaret Thatcher, 81

Mariah Carey, 171

Marie Curie, 162, 201

Mario Andretti, 162

Mark Spitz, 88

Mark Twain, 29, 31, 39, 122, 145, 151, 162, 169, 172, 194, 227, 257, 278, 286, 299

Mark Victor Hansen, 101, 122, 212

Mark Zupan, 88

Marlene Dietrich, 3

Marshall Field, 237

Martha Stewart, 270

Martin Luther King, Jr., 61, 122, 162, 186, 276, 296

Martina Navratilova, 77

Mary Kay Ash, 122

Mary Lou Retton, 129

Maya Angelou, 190

Meister Eckhart, 293

Melody Beattie, 293

Mia Hamm, 66

Michael Caine, 88

Michael Harrington, 69

Michael Jordan, 112, 122, 162, 183, 207, 243

Michael Korda, 231, 308, 310

Michael LeBoeuf, 257

Michael Phelps, 162, 213

Michelangelo, 102, 206

Mickey Rooney, 39

Miguel De Cervantes, 170

Mike Davidson, 235

Mike Ditka, 162

Mike Leavitt, 177

Milton Berle, 266

Miyamoto Musashi, 83, 122, 163, 206

Mohandas Gandhi, 18, 145, 146, 233, 263, 296

Morihei Ueshiba, 183

Morrie Schwartz, 146

Mother Teresa, 57, 280, 290

Muhammad Ali, 88, 102, 138, 146, 219

Napoleon Bonaparte, 39, 122, 183, 249

Napoleon Hill, 40, 44, 57, 61, 67, 81, 102, 107, 116, 122, 163, 183, 201, 213, 219, 227, 267, 291

Nathaniel Branden, 146

Neal Boortz, 40

Nelson Boswell, 237

Nelson Mandela, 69

Newt Gingrich, 163

Niccolo Machiavelli, 266

Nicholas Sparks, 280

Nido Qubein, 19, 27, 83, 102, 146, 190

Nike Sneaker Company, 123

Nolan Bushnell, 123

THE SUCCESS FORMULA FOR PERSONAL GROWTH

Nolan Ryan, 190

Nora Roberts, 40

Norman R. Augustine, 168

Norman Vincent Peale, 57, 70, 78, 81, 92, 112, 132, 146, 177, 194, 201, 213, 227, 286

Og Mandino, 19, 40, 48, 52, 62, 78, 83, 102, 109, 123, 129, 132, 146, 152, 163, 183, 201, 232, 258, 286, 291, 308, 312, 314

Ogden Nash, 304

Oliver Wendall Holmes, Jr., 27

Oprah Winfrey, 33, 40, 48, 57, 67, 83, 103, 129, 138, 152, 170, 175, 183, 194, 201, 263, 282, 288, 304, 308, 310

Orison Swett Marden, 19, 78, 112, 129, 258, 304

Orville Wright, 273

Oscar Wilde, 70, 152, 296, 312

P. T. Barnum, 83, 129

Pablo Picasso, 19, 29, 123, 210, 315

Pamela Anderson, 239

Pat Croce, 26, 31, 34, 40, 48, 67, 70, 78, 84, 92, 95, 103, 112, 117, 132, 152, 164, 194, 220, 227, 243, 258, 273, 282, 302, 304, 314

Pat Riley, 9, 48, 78, 109, 152, 243, 276

Patrick Dixon, 258

Paul (Bear) Bryant, 183

Paul Harvey, 67

Paul Meyer, 19

Pele, 133

Pete Rose, 88

Peter Drucker, 109, 175, 186, 190, 227, 235, 238, 249, 258

Peter McWilliams, 183, 233

Phil Jackson, 190

Philip Armour, 249

Plato, 227

Pope John XXIII, 27

Publilius Syrus, 58, 117

Pythagoras, 213

Ralph Waldo Emerson, 58, 70, 73, 103, 133, 147, 164, 201, 210, 278, 291, 292, 302, 308

Ray Kroc, 249, 308

Red Skelton, 287

Rene Descartes, 152, 178

Reuben Gonzalez, 278

Richard Back, 49

Richard Branson, 270

Richard M. DeVos, 62, 152

Rita Coolidge, 267

Robert Burns, 117

Robert Collier, 123, 147, 216, 249, 267

Robert F. Kennedy, 138

Robert G. Allen, 259, 305

Robert J. Ringer, 84, 88, 92

Robert Kiyosaki, 23, 26, 70, 138, 178, 305

Robert Louis Stevenson, 28

Robert R. Updegraff, 287

Robin S. Sharma, 259

Roger Bannister, 164
Roger Maris, 88
Roger Smith, 31
Roger Staubach, 88
Roger Von Oech, 40, 183, 273
Rollo May, 278
Ronald Reagan, 263
Rosa Parks, 201
Ross Perot, 164
Roy H. Williams, 23
Ruben Gonzalez, 164, 216
Rudyard Kipling, 44
Russell H. Ewing, 249
Russell Simmons, 40, 78, 273
Russian Proverb, 259
Saint Augustine, 165
Saint Ignatius Loyola, 259
Sam Levenson, 2
Sam Silverstein, 44
Sam Walton, 113, 238, 250
Samuel Johnson, 52, 164, 298
Samuel Smiles, 40, 70, 73, 113, 147, 184, 259, 267
Sean (Puff Daddy) Combs, 70
Sebastian Coe, 207
Seneca, 41
Serena and Venus Williams, 89, 164
Seth Godin, 211
Shakti Gawain, 49, 216, 219
Sidney J. Harris, 299
Smiley Blanton, 129
Socrates, 31
Soichiro Honda, 184
Sophocles, 3, 184
Stan Smith, 147
Steve Bennett, 19, 250
Steve Garvey, 103
Steve Jobs, 31, 67, 84, 184
Steven Covey, 26, 28, 31, 49, 62, 138, 147, 168, 184, 194, 217, 227, 259, 287
Steven Hawking, 190
Sun Tzu, 267
Susan Polis Schutz, 103
Suze Orman, 306
Sven Goran Eriksson, 201
Sydney Smith, 280
Sylvester Stallone, 204
T. Boone Pickens, 175
Ted Williams, 103
Terry Bradshaw, 109
Terry Cole-Whittaker, 194
The Talmud, 3
Theodore Isaac Rubin, 178
Theodore Roosevelt, 70, 92, 147, 202, 243
Thomas Carlyle, 103, 147
Thomas Edison, 26, 67, 165, 184, 267, 273, 278, 312
Thomas Fuller, 44, 165, 297
Thomas J. Watson, 78
Thomas Jefferson, 129, 152, 227, 282, 300, 308
Thomas Merton, 70

Thomas S. Monson, 126, 283
Thomas S. Szasz, 297
Tiger Woods, 67
Tom Landry, 103
Tom Peters, 235, 238, 240, 250
Tommy Lasorda, 165
Tony Alessandra, 232, 276
Tony Blair, 250
Tony Dorsett, 168
Tony Robbins, 20, 23, 26, 28, 34, 41, 49, 53, 62, 67, 70, 73, 78, 84, 92, 95, 104, 109, 123, 129, 136, 175, 178, 184, 194, 202, 204, 228, 260, 276, 288, 302, 312, 315
Tyra Banks, 129
Venus Williams, 153
Victor Hugo, 136, 280
Vilfredo Pareto, 260
Vince Lombardi, 20, 53, 78, 81, 89, 92, 110, 130, 147, 165, 172, 195, 243, 250
Virgil, 147
Virginia Satir, 172
Voltaire, 2, 41, 178, 251, 315
W. Clement Stone, 28, 50, 58, 104, 124, 153, 166, 172, 185, 187, 202, 219, 283, 287, 315
W. Edwards Deming, 126, 315
W. Timothy Gallwey, 84
W.H. Murray, 110
Wally (Famous) Amos, 148
Walt Disney, 71, 238, 278
Walter Winchel, 170
Warren Buffet, 23, 276, 306
Wayne Dyer, 28, 49, 58, 124, 148, 166, 168, 195, 208
Wayne Gretzky, 41, 190
Wendell Barry, 2
Whoopi Goldberg, 62
Will Rogers, 20, 117, 124, 138, 228
Will Smith, 306
William B. Sprague, 139
William DeMille, 71
William E. Hickson, 166
William Faulkner, 124
William H. Johnson, 41
William James, 63, 85, 153
William Osler, 89, 310
William Penn, 291
William Shakespeare, 41
William Wordsworth, 263
Willie Nelson, 196
Willis Harman, 58
Winston Churchill, 3, 92, 153, 166, 185, 278, 289
Yogi Berra, 243
Zen Proverb, 79
Zig Ziglar, 20, 28, 41, 50, 53, 81, 89, 92, 104, 117, 124, 148, 153, 166, 168, 185, 190, 196, 217, 228, 232, 260, 276, 306

Made in the USA
Lexington, KY
01 February 2011